OUT OF THE 4TH PLACE

IF YOU DON'T LIKE WHAT CHURCH HAS BECOME...
THERE IS A BETTER WAY

OUT OF THE 4TH PLACE

MATT BROWELEIT with DUDLEY CALLISON

BACK DECK BOOKS
SEATTLE, WA

Cover design and cover and interior illustrations by Robin Renard

First Printing, 2018

To obtain permissions or to order books (including special rates for bulk purchases) visit www.outofthe4thplace.com.

Back Deck Books
Seattle, WA 98155
www.outofthe4thplace.com

To Katie, I love you.

The best things are created in community. Thank you to everyone who took part in reading and refining my writing. Here's to rich conversation, gentle mocking and fresh perspective.

Katie Broweleit, Tim Isaacson, Larry Broweleit, Jon Koetje, Pam Wenz, Jason Bosh, Kelley Higgs, John Lewis, Dr. Sam Rima, Josh Henning, Mike Makalusky, Jenny Tabert, Carolyn Threadgill, Chris Kennedy, Dr. Craig Blomberg, Brandon Hare, David Katz, Chris Kopp, Rabbi Matt Rosenberg, Rob Karch, Mike Labrum, Trent Siverson, Daniel Steigerwald, Michael Kuder

Special thanks and love to my kids, Annabelle, Lizzy, Andrew and Mia, who have lived this conversation from birth.

CONTENTS

PART 1 · INTO THE 4TH PLACE

PART 2 · THE 4TH PLACE TODAY

PART 3 · OUT OF THE 4TH PLACE

PART 1

INTO THE 4TH PLACE

1

The Medium Is the Message

The *third place* is somewhere between home and work. Starbucks is a *third place*. In fact, that was the whole point. Howard Schultz was so inspired by the coffee culture of Italy that he wanted to share it with America. And it wasn't just the superior espresso. It was the environment surrounding the espresso—the laughter, community and romance of the Italian *piazza*. Schultz didn't just want people to enjoy a cappuccino, he wanted them to taste the flavor of the *third place*.[1]

Third Place Books in Seattle is among my favorite spots to connect with people, grab a bite to eat or discover a new book.

Where did this term, *third place*, come from? Sociologist Ray Oldenburg invented it and wrote about it in his book, *The Great Good Place*. According to Oldenburg's model, the *first place* is the home— *private life*.

---

[1]"Company Information." Starbucks. Accessed October 15, 2015. http://www.starbucks.com/about-us/company-information.

The *second place* is work or school—*productive life*. The *third place* is where we go to unwind. It's what Oldenburg calls *informal public life*. He writes:

> Great civilizations, like great cities, share a common feature. Evolving within them and crucial to their growth and refinement are distinctive informal public gathering places. These become as much a part of the urban landscape as of the citizen's daily life, and invariably, they come to dominate the image of the city. Thus, its profusion of sidewalk cafés seems to *be* Paris, just as The Forum dominates one's mental picture of classic Rome. The soul of London resides in her many pubs; that of Florence in its teeming *piazzas*.[2]

Maybe you have a favorite pub. A coffee shop you like to frequent. A park. We go to *third places* to laugh, to get lost in the music, to sip on something fantastic. We all understand *third places*. They are a welcome part of our life.

But I'm not writing about *third places*. I'm writing about church. Where do church buildings fit into Oldenburg's model?

Are they *first places*? No.

Are they *second places*? Only for church employees.

Are they *third places*? No, people don't usually go to church buildings just to hang out. They go there for scheduled events.

So...where do churches fit? Hint: they don't.

Churches are part of the *fourth place*.

---

[2] Ray Oldenburg, *The Great Good Place* (Cambridge, MA: Da Capo, 1989), xxviii.

And just to get it out of the way early, that's not a good thing for the church. It's actually quite a large problem. Being in the *fourth place* is part of the reason churches are misusing resources, millennials are leaving, and pastors are burning out. I'll explain why in a minute.

First, I want to address the obvious question, "What in the world is the *fourth place*?" If the *third place* is *informal public life*, then there must be a fourth category, *formal public life*. You can't have the category *informal* without its counterpart category *formal*, so I am adding a category to the model: *formal public life*—the *fourth place*.

The *fourth place*, then, would include such institutions as country clubs, temples, stadiums, and yes, churches. Where else would any of these fit in Oldenburg's model? Nowhere. They are *fourth places*, formal public institutions—places of insiders and outsiders, those with tickets and those without. If you have ever wondered why your church felt like a country club, this is likely the reason.

For some of you the wheels are already turning and you are already thinking about all of the issues in the church that might be explained by us being in the *fourth place*. That's good and we'll talk a lot about that. Others might be thinking, "Okay, so what? Yes, we're in the *fourth place*. Isn't that where churches belong? Isn't that normal?" Though it may feel completely normal, we only think so because we are so accustomed to it.

The Wrong Place

Why is being in the *fourth place* such a big issue? For starters, because Jesus intentionally moved church *out of the fourth place*. Remember the Old Testament temple? It was a big building that people went to in order to worship God. The temple was a *fourth place*.

Jesus changed that. Jesus *is* the temple. Remember, when he said, "Destroy this temple and I'll raise it in three days" (John 2:19), Jesus wasn't talking about a building. He was talking about his body. In other words, Jesus took something that used to be a *fourth place*, the physical temple, and he moved it right into the normal rhythms of his culture. The temple became human and walked around the neighborhood.

Not only did Jesus move the church out of the *fourth place*, so did the early church. The early church didn't have their own place. They had no temples or other religious buildings. And not just because of persecution—we'll talk about that in Chapter 3. They self-identified as exiles, strangers, a people without a place of their own. Persecution was certainly a part of it, but they actually stayed in culture on purpose. Just like Jesus.

The early church lived and gathered within culture, not separate from it. They met in *first places*—homes. They met in *second places*—workspaces, farms, shops, military camps. They met in *third places*—river banks, theaters, catacombs. Solomon's Colonnade, where they met in Acts, was a busy place full of people coming and going. It was both a *second* and a *third place*.

If Jesus and the early church avoided the *fourth place*, why is it so normal for us?

Now don't worry. If you think I am just going to offer the solution, "We all need to read Acts 2:42 and sell our buildings," that's not where I'm going. I am not going to argue that we simply copy the early church. A lot of books do that. But times have changed. Cultures have changed. It's not just a building thing. Can our buildings be part of the problem? Of course. But the problem is much more complex and interesting than that.

Why is church in the *fourth place* such a big problem?

Why write a book on it?

Here is why: the *fourth place* is preaching messages to our world that we would never want to say with our mouths.

The Medium Is the Message

Perhaps you have heard the principle, *the medium is the message*. Marshall McLuhan, a professor and early media theory expert, coined this phrase in the 1960s.[3] It means that the form, or medium, that contains a message often speaks louder than the message itself.

Medium can refer to art. For example, a sculpture will by its very nature speak a different message from a watercolor painting. *Medium* can also refer to types of technology. Television will communicate differently from print media. A tweet is different from a conversation.

The medium is the message isn't just about art and technology. All kinds of media can affect the messages we hear. The word "relax" sounds different during a massage than during a colonoscopy. I respond differently to the words "trust me" when coming from my loving wife than coming from a used car salesman. A contract isn't as firm when signed with a pink glitter pen. A steak isn't as fine when served on a paper plate.

You get it. The medium dramatically impacts the message. It may even overshadow the message. It may even *be* its own message.

This same principle applies to our churches. Pastors will spend hours, even days, crafting a single sermon, but may not be thinking about the "sermon" the forms themselves are preaching. What message do people hear when they drive past the church facility? What about when they see how people dress? What about when they see who is on stage? What does having a stage in the first place say?

---

[3] Marshall McLuhan and Quentin Fiore, *The Medium is the Massage* (New York: Bantam Books, 1967).

Now maybe you are a pastor, maybe you are a student, maybe you attend a church, or maybe you have lost interest in church. Regardless of where you are coming from, most of us have some level of interest in the messages of our churches. We want our messages to speak of Jesus. To reflect him. To help people understand him.

But what messages are people actually hearing? What is the *fourth place* saying behind all of the songs and sermons?

I want to suggest in this book that we have a big problem, probably bigger than we realize. I want to suggest that our mouths are preaching the greatest messages in the history of the world: reconciliation with God, restored community with each other, purpose in the world.

Our forms, however, are often preaching the exact opposite messages: separation from God, separation from each other, separation from the world.

Why? Because the medium is the message. Whenever you put religion in the *fourth place* it will automatically start speaking for itself. And it will sound just like a temple.

Remember, Jesus moved the church out of the temple—*out of the fourth place*. Unfortunately, the church moved back in. When did that happen? How did we move back into the *fourth place*?

I will explain this in detail in Chapter 4, but the short answer is that in fourth century Rome, Constantine helped to rebuild the temple of stone that Jesus had turned to flesh. When Constantine made Christianity the official religion of the Roman Empire, he rebuilt Christianity not as a living temple scattered throughout all of the cultures of the world, but instead as a place of its own religious culture. Rather than expressing the beauty and diversity of the cultures of the world, the church would express the culture of the *fourth place*.

Christianity changed. What used to reflect the life and love of Jesus now looked more like Rome. They only spoke Latin—in France. They wore hot robes—in Africa. It wasn't all Constantine's fault; the change was gradual and in fact, was already happening before he came to power. Christendom then took the torch and built on Constantine's foundation for century upon century. It's a complicated history. Regardless, Christianity changed. It moved out of the *first*, *second* and *third places* and back into the *fourth place*. A religious place. A place of political power. A place of its own culture, language, strange hair styles and cheesy music.

Constantine placed the church into a category it was never meant to occupy; the *fourth place—formal public life*. Most religions have temples. Temples are religious buildings where people go to do religious activities. That is how most religions work. That is how the Old Testament temple worked. But not the New Testament temple. Christianity was supposed to be different. We were supposed to be the temple of the Holy Spirit. We were supposed to be a living temple. A temple that lived among its culture like exiles, like strangers, like salt and light in the world.

We even say these things with our mouths in our services. "You, people, are the temple. You are the dwelling place of God. You, congregation, are the church." The problem is not so much what we are saying with our mouths. The real problem is that our medium is speaking its own message. We are not doing it intentionally. We usually don't even realize we are doing it.

Outsiders are noticing. They know we don't look or sound much like Jesus. What if they are right?

What if our words are telling people to love their neighbors, but our forms are telling them to fear them?

What if we are telling our people we care about the poor, but our media are telling them we mostly care about the beautiful and talented?

What if we are preaching grace but our forms are preaching legalism?

What if we are telling people to be disciples but our forms are telling them to be consumers?

Is it possible that all of these disconnects are the primary reason people—especially millennials—no longer trust the church? What if these mixed messages are the main reason that pastors and church leaders are getting frustrated, struggling and burning out? Would that matter to you? I hope so. It really matters to me. That's why I am finally writing this book. I resisted for a long time, but felt compelled. My friends, mentors and I thought this message was worth sharing.

My Background

I'm guessing you have never heard my name before. Reading something from a no-name can be a bit risky. I confess I rarely do it myself. I am not going to try to impress anyone with my resume. In fact, you will find as you read this book that I believe celebrity leaders are part of the problem, not the solution. But I want to give you some of my background so you know the variety of experiences that are informing this book.

I am a father of four and a husband to the best wife ever. I live a mentored life and a life in community. I am an artist and a thinker. I try my best by God's grace to practice the things I am convinced matter.

I went to public school in Seattle and an extremely liberal university. I am used to being a person with more conservative values and theology in a world sometimes hostile to those ideas. It is natural for me to build relationships across racial, denominational and political lines. After college I lived in and helped run a home to transition homeless and addicted men back into life. I have spent significant time in "secular" professions, including seven years in technology at an investment company.

I graduated from Denver Seminary with a Masters of Divinity degree, though I have yet to master any divinity. I like to study and read broadly from many perspectives. I have worked in churches for many years— leading worship, preaching and teaching groups of all sizes—small, medium and megachurches. Some have been charismatic congregations, some evangelical (whatever that means anymore), and some more liturgical. All these perspectives have given me a passion for unity in the body and a deep sense of grief over our division.

I have also helped to start churches outside of the building-centered context. Authors in the missional dialogue, justice movement and spiritual formation resonate with me particularly.

Most importantly, I love Jesus. I love the Bible. And I love the church.

Why write a book?

Because through all these experiences, I continue to see the same patterns and issues emerge over and over again. I have watched, served, studied, read, discussed and prayed. And I have come to some conclusions.

A Systems Issue

Many people assume there are quick fixes to the types of issues I have brought up. Millennials are leaving? Culture hates you? Just preach better sermons. Hire a new pastor who gets it. We simply need a worship leader who is relevant. We need a bigger building. Better programs. More staff. Greater tithing.

It's not that simple.

Before working full-time for churches, I worked for a company called Russell Investments. On my team we had a policy that when a big mistake was made, our team would sit down and dig into the issue together. We wanted total transparency so we could fix it. We put problems in two main categories—human error and systems issues. When it was a one-time problem, there was a decent chance it was a human error. Maybe we needed to coach our employees better. Maybe we needed a new team member. However, when the problem occurred over and over again, there was a better chance that it was a systems issue—a problem in the underlying computer code, a process that was broken, a structural problem.

The types of issues we are experiencing in the church are systems-level issues. They are not isolated events. There are patterns. Pastors are burning out at alarming rates. Staff members are having affairs. The church feels fake. There is alarmingly poor allocation of resources toward community needs. People are consistently being used and hurt.

These are not "preach a better sermon" nor "hire the right pastor" types of issues. We are experiencing a systems-level epidemic and we need to treat it as such.

Many great books, blogs and curricula are being thrown into the discussion to figure out what is going on and what to do about it. This book is my small attempt to add a simple idea into this ongoing dialogue.

I am convinced that a major player in the discussion needs to be the disconnect between our medium and our message. We are trying to follow an incarnate Christ from the *fourth place*. We are attempting to live out a gospel of reconciliation on a church platform of separation.

And it isn't working.

Nagging Questions

We have a lot of issues as a church in the West. Maybe you relate with some of the questions and concerns I am bringing up. Maybe you have experienced the painful fruit of these issues for yourself. For me, the questions just won't go away. Way back in college, I started feeling that something was off, but it began to come to a head after graduation.

I went to the University of Puget Sound in Tacoma, Washington. Six other guys and I were in a small group for all four of those years. We were part of a wonderful ministry called Lighthouse. Our group of friends was so tight that we decided to continue to meet together after college. Eventually, we all got married, started having kids, and moved into an urban Tacoma neighborhood within a few blocks of each other. We wanted to see if we could continue some of our college community experience and also make an impact on our little part of the city.

It wasn't always easy, but the plan actually worked. We served neighbors, threw block parties, hung out a lot, studied the Bible and poured our lives into a local public elementary school. We intentionally shared life and mission. In the process, we saw abused kids receive hope, races intermingle and some neighbors meet Jesus.

At the same time, I was leading worship at a local church. None of our neighborhood friends was a part of that church. I was living in two church worlds—my neighborhood world and my worship-leading world.

And I started to have so many questions.

Why are we spending so much time and money on big events at church when I see so much more lasting fruit from a neighborhood block party?

Why do I feel like my neighborhood life is building up my family while my church life is tearing me away from them?

Why am I working so hard for great musical productions while half of the team's marriages are blowing up?

Why do I feel like we're using people for their talents but don't have time to care about their real life?

Why am I spending so much time in this building when the people we're trying to reach are outside of it?

I hear from people all the time who are wrestling with the same types of questions. I myself went to Denver Seminary to study them. I processed them through my years as a small groups pastor at a megachurch. I read everything I could get my hands on related to the topic. Today, I am still wrestling with the questions, but I have also come to some clarity; thus this book.

I am convinced that a large part of the problem is connected to our *fourth place* medium. We are using temple structures to run a relational church. And they are at odds like oil and water.

Who Is This Book For?

If any of the questions I have asked resonate with your experience, this book is for you.

Maybe you are a church planter and are dreaming and praying about how and where to start. A major focus of the book is planting churches based outside of the *fourth place*. How do you plant churches in the *first*, *second* and *third* places of culture? We will talk at length about this new paradigm and examples of where it is already being practiced in the world today.

Maybe you are an existing church pastor, worship leader or staff member. Chances are, you have already felt the need as a church to simplify, focus on small groups or missional communities, and help people grow as disciples in their world. This book will expand what you are already doing, give you language to help you talk about your challenges and perhaps take you several steps beyond what you were already planning.

Maybe you used to like church and have become a bit disillusioned with the whole thing. You like Jesus but struggle with his followers, the institution or the politics. This book will help you process your frustration and perhaps even find hope again.

Maybe you work with a parachurch organization and are concerned with the partnership between church and parachurch. This book will explain why you feel this and what we can do about it.

Maybe you aren't even a Christian, but wonder why Jesus seems so amazing but Christians give you the heebie-jeebies—like they are part of some strange subculture. This book will help you understand the disconnect.

This book is for anyone who wants to understand the purpose of church, how we veered from Jesus, and how we can get back again.

Where Are We Going?

We are going on a journey of church media; church forms.

PART 1 of the book will explain how we got into the *fourth place*. If we are going to get out of the *fourth place* we need to understand how we got there.

You may be tempted to skip Part 1, but I'd encourage you to dig deep through these early chapters. Chapters 2, 3 and 4 are critical. You might not realize how deeply we are affected by temple forms and how much Christendom plays into everything we do today.

The first chapters will challenge your understanding of the Bible and will build the theological foundations we need for the rest of the book.

You may be surprised that even long-time students of scripture will find they have been interpreting it through the lens of the *fourth place*. Prepare to be stretched.

PART 2 of the book is deconstruction time. Here we come to grips with the impact of the *fourth place* on the modern church. It affects everything we do. In order to understand the solutions we first need to understand the extent of the problems. And sometimes it gets a little ugly. However, while Part 2 deconstructs and points some fingers, it also gives hope.

All of us are starting from different places—different types of churches, polity, structure and liturgy. Each of the chapters in Part 2 will help you to identify your own unique starting point so you know with clarity what it looks like for you to move out of the *fourth place*.

PART 3 contains some solutions. How do we get out of the *fourth place* and what exactly does life look like once we are out? We will discover that our churches have often been designed for the wrong function, or purpose. We will unpack the true function of church and the forms that will help us accomplish that purpose.

When I read a book like this, I always want to know a little about where we are going before I can commit. So, at risk of giving away some of what is to come, I want to give you a short summary of what the solutions look like.

Again, the solutions are not simple. The problems are enormous. Regardless, the following graphics will help us understand a framework for how to move forward.

You will get familiar with this chart as we go along. The little church building in the top left corner is sitting in the *fourth place*. That's the top left quadrant—where we do our thing, in our place.

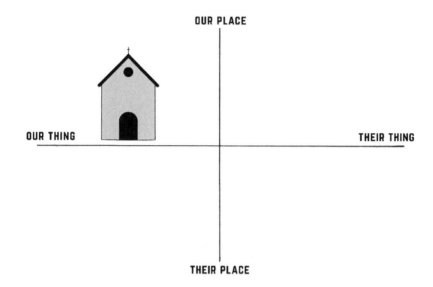

You will notice that there are two lines, or axes, on this chart, **PLACES** and **THINGS**. **PLACES** refers to **WHERE** we do what we do. The top half is the church building. I simply call it OUR PLACE because we own it and that's where we do our religious gatherings. The bottom half is THEIR PLACE, the *first*, *second* and *third* places of culture—the places we all live, eat, sleep, work and play.

THINGS refers to **WHO** is running it. If our church is running it, then it's OUR THING. If it's something the rest of the culture is doing, it's THEIR THING.

The church in this chart is in the OUR THING, OUR PLACE quadrant because that's where we're used to it being. For most people in the West, this is how we see church. It is OUR PLACE where we do OUR THING. Church is an event in a building. A religious place for religious activities. Just like a temple. But like we said, that's not where Jesus put us. Jesus put church here:

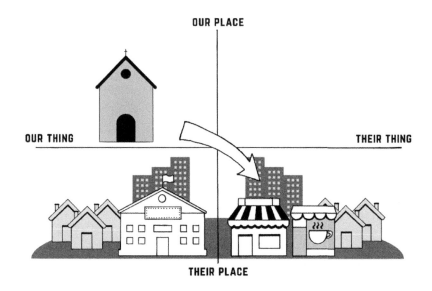

Jesus took the temple and he moved it into culture. The temple became flesh. So, how do we get out of the *fourth place*? Do we just throw out the building? Do we scrap the institution—as if the church needs no structure or organization? It depends where you are starting from. We will present two major pathways forward.

1. Out of the Fourth Place

If you are starting from scratch, we will spend a lot of time talking about planting and maturing churches outside of the *fourth place*. This does not mean church without buildings. It means church without *religious* buildings.

If you are ready for something a little more radical and less like the traditional church, we want to provide you with a map for what that can look like. To help guide the discussion of new church media I have asked my good friend and mentor, Dudley Callison, former President of Communitas International, to help us. Communitas is a global missional church planting organization; many of the churches they've planted exist in culture without their own religious buildings. These churches do not lack structure; they simply use a fundamentally *different* structure. Dudley will contribute his experiences and stories from the many missional initiatives, church plants and mature communities that are a part of their movement.

Communitas plants churches globally, including in the Americas, but primarily in post-Christian Western Europe. In other words, they are used to planting churches where people don't like church. Therefore, they are ahead of the learning curve for what the culture is quickly becoming in the United States. Dudley will not only contribute stories to Part 3, but will also comment along the way in the earlier chapters so that we continually mix real world application with the theological framework we are developing.

Two Expressions
by Dudley Callison

Growing up in suburban Dallas culture, I participated in two expressions of church. Park Cities Baptist Church was easy to identify. It has a large campus with beautiful architecture, a loving staff and effective programs. This "static" version of church helped me grow in faith and I'm truly thankful. I also participated in my high school Young Life club. We worshipped Christ together and we shared in authentic community. Maybe most importantly, we were organized around a shared sense of mission—to reach our peers at school who would never show up at church. We didn't ever call Young Life our church, but for many kids it was the only version of church they could relate to. It was their spiritual family. It was mine too, and it did more to shape my future understanding of "dynamic" church planting in the post-Christendom world than I could have ever imagined.

2. Repurposing the Fourth Place

If you are starting with an existing building, we will talk about how any church can take incremental steps toward integration and away from separation. There are three main directions for growth that you can apply without selling the facility. Here they are:

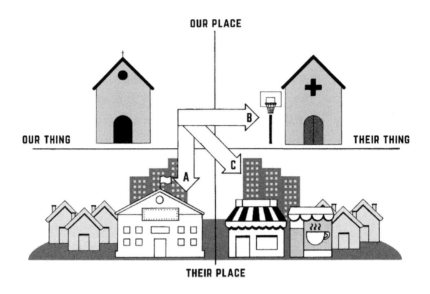

Chances are you have moved in one or more of these directions already without even knowing about the *fourth place.*

A. Maybe you started small groups or missional communities and you got people meeting in homes. Maybe you're doing a venue church or meeting in a school. Those are movements along **Arrow A.**

B. Maybe you are converting your *fourth place* into a *first, second* or *third place.* If your church opened a public coffee shop or gym, you just opened a *third place.* If you have tenants working out of your building, you just opened a *second place.* Maybe you are housing the homeless or renting out parts of your building for income. You just created a *first place.* Maybe your church building doesn't look like a church building. Your building is a functional hospital, warehouse, office building or community center. If your building includes *first*, *second* or *third* places, you are moving in the direction of **Arrow B.**

C. Finally, maybe you are simplifying the Sunday event so that you can better walk with people in the context of real life. You are helping people learn to take responsibility in their own world to care for their neighbors. You are helping people live like Christ in the workplace.

Now I'm not just talking about preaching on those topics. That's a fine start, but I'm talking about your media—staff time and resources. What does this look like practically? It means you are structured at least in part like a parachurch ministry. Young Life, InterVarsity and others work in coffee shops, spend intentional time at schools, and treat the normal lives of people as if they are worth spending ministry time and money investing in. If you are engaging with people in their world on purpose you are moving down **Arrow C.**

This is a high-level summary and I am throwing a lot at you quickly. Don't worry, we will explain all of this in depth and provide many examples for what this looks like. Whether you are ready for radically new forms or whether you want to apply the principles at a slower pace to an existing system, this book will provide the direction you need to move forward.

There are several ways out of the *fourth place*. Some involve ditching the building or meeting in a non-religious space. Others involve repurposing the building, the job description or the worship service. All involve becoming more like Christ in the world.

When Jesus came to earth he left his own place. He entered our world. Maybe it's time that we follow him there. Maybe it's time to get *out of the fourth place*.

2

Fourth Place Technology

There was a day when the desktop PC lived at the center of the computing universe. Bill Gates sat on the throne. Steve Jobs was a has-been. Network administrators had job security. Car phones were only for society's elite. The cloud was just a white puffy thing in the sky.

Then along came the mobile device. The iPod and iPhone put Apple back on the map. A couple of college kids started a little company called Google. Jeff Bezos began selling some books online at a website named after a South American river. The paradigm began to shift—the world was going mobile.

Work used to take place at a desk. Not *any* desk. No, a *particular* desk. The one with your computer at it with your information saved on it. If you wanted to get something done, you needed to go to that *particular* desk.

No working from home. No sitting in a coffee shop to work remotely.

When the PC reigned, work was tethered, centered. When we went mobile, work went everywhere. At home. In the car. At *any* desk. And what happened to work happened in every sphere of society.

Communication used to be centered. Voices used to travel over wires into homes. If you wanted to talk you needed to be within ten feet of the phone. Why? Communication only went as far as the length of the cord. Commerce used to be centered. Consumers had to physically drive to a store and pick out their purchases. No one-step clicking, or swiping, or Prime, or having a package magically show up on your doorstep.

When we went mobile, the center was gone. What does this have to do with church? Everything.

Everywhere Worship

In the Garden of Eden there was no center to worship. Worship was mobile. There were no physical temples in Eden. Worship didn't have a *particular* place. Worship had *every* place. Worship was integrated into all of life. God is omnipresent—everywhere at all times. Wherever Adam and Eve walked in the garden, there was worship. Wherever Adam and Eve worked, there was worship. Wherever Adam and Eve played, ate, sang, loved and laughed, there was worship.

Worship needed no physical temple. No *fourth place*. No center. Adam and Eve were continually connected.

With God.
With each other.
With the creation itself.

In the beginning there was no division between sacred and secular. No Christian music versus non-Christian music. There was just music. Non-qualified music. There were no holy buildings. Garden, mountain and river were all holy. There were no priests; no one was closer to God than anyone else.

In Eden, we didn't need religious activities to please God. Work pleased God. Sex pleased God. Taking care of the natural environment pleased God. And he called it all *good*. All of life was **integrated**. All of life was worship because every sphere of life was connected to God and aligned with him, the source of life.

But then we lost our connection.

Connection Dropped

Mobile phones rely on radio waves and a very small antenna. Your phone takes all of that digital data you send out—emails, texts, tweets, your mom's cat videos—and converts it to an electrical signal that can be transmitted over radio waves. Everything comes and goes via your antenna. You can't see it on most modern phones, but it's there—a small antenna picking up the signal, sending and receiving data at the speed of light.

Adam and Eve were connected to God. Deeply connected. Intimately connected. When they sinned, the connection was lost.

The antenna, broken.

As C.S. Lewis would remind us, metaphors always break down at some point. To compare the connection to God in Eden with our connection via technology is a helpful image, but grossly inadequate.

We may feel connected to the world through our devices but it is nothing compared to the deep and intimate connection of Adam and Eve to their creator. We may feel "naked" without a phone, but it is nothing compared to the nakedness Adam and Eve felt that moment the connection was lost.

Can you imagine a pure connection to the God of the universe? Can you imagine the safety and love of human relationships with absolutely pure motives? Can you imagine meaningful work without the thorns?

That is what we had. All of it. But as soon as we had it, we lost it. When we lost our connection through sin, we lost the signal. We were separated—holy from unholy, sacred from secular.

The connection to God—turned to shame.
The connection to each other—replaced with competition.
The connection to creation—ruined by thorn and injustice.

Genesis 3:24 states, "After he drove the man out, he placed on the east side of the Garden of Eden cherubim and a flaming sword flashing back and forth to guard the way to the tree of life."

God placed cherubim to guard the way back to life.

God's Pursuit of Relationship

God never changes. His desire for us never decreases. His love is unending, immeasurable, incalculable. It wasn't that God stopped transmitting the signal; it's that our antennas were damaged beyond repair. The radio waves of his presence were still everywhere, but nobody could tune in.

So what did God do?

Did he give up on humanity? Did he leave us alone in our isolation? No, he pursued us. He appeared to Abraham and spoke. He called one nation out of all of the nations of the earth. He chose them and delivered them from Egypt. He chose a place for his dwelling—fire, a cloud, a tabernacle, finally the temple in Jerusalem. An ark. A room with a curtain.

He gave people with broken antennas ways to tune in. Since they couldn't be with him in the garden he made himself available here: the *fourth place.*

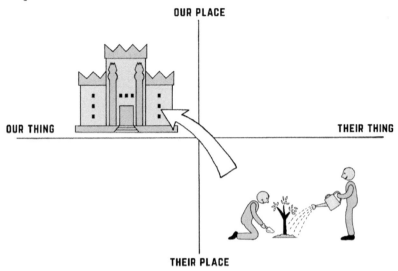

After all, how do you communicate with people when the mobile connection goes down? You choose a *particular* place. If the cell towers fell and we became disconnected, we would be forced to revert to life before the cloud. If you are having visions of the 1980s, big hair and fantastic music, you are not far off. We would have to return to the era of the desktop PC. Software. Discs. Networking people plugging ethernet cables into wall ports.

Our information would be limited to a particular place. In order to compute things, we would have to go to the desk again. Not just any desk. No, the *particular* desk—the one that has the computer tower with our files saved on it. Why? Because loss of a mobile connection necessitates particular places.

In Eden there were no temples, no religious *fourth places.* And when we turn to the back of the book and catch a glimpse of the new heavens and the new earth in Revelation there are still no temples. John writes in his Revelation that in the eternal city he saw no temple (Rev. 21:22). The glory of God will be everywhere. It will be a new and fully integrated creation.

So then, if the temple is missing from the bookends of the creation and the Revelation, then we need to ask the question, *why do temples appear in the middle of the story?*[4]

The Need for the Fourth Place

Only God in his wisdom knows all of his reasons, but at one level the temple existed because the antenna was broken and God chose a way to temporarily restore our lost connection.

The everywhere worship of Eden was lost, so God chose a *particular* place: Jerusalem, the Temple Mount.

The temple was an act of love. Throughout scripture we hear the refrain, "I will be their God and they will be my people."[5] The temple represents God's relentless pursuit of his creation. However, in the midst of this pursuit we also feel a tension. While the medium of the temple represented God's loving desire to be with his creation, it also represented the reality of the broken relationship. Embedded into the forms of the temple were reminders of the integrated life of worship in Eden that was lost.

---

[4] It is important to realize that Jesus is, was, and will always be the temple. Jesus never changes. At the end of the story, John says in Revelation 21:22, "I did not see a temple in the city, because the Lord God Almighty and the Lamb are its temple." God himself is the temple. In Eden, the temple existed. At the end of the story, the temple will still exist. The difference is the manifestation of the temple. When I say, there was no temple in Eden nor in the new heavens and the new earth, I am referring to no *physical* temple of stone or bricks or wood— no building set apart as the place to encounter God.

[5] Jer. 31:31, Ezek. 11:20, 2 Cor. 6:16, Heb. 8:10

In Eden humanity walked with God in the garden, enjoying his presence wherever they went. In the temple, however, God limited his presence to one room, the Holy of Holies. In Eden God was accessible to everyone, but in the temple only one tribe could access the holiest places—the Levites. Only one man could enter the Holy of Holies—the High Priest. One man. No women. We even see the same cherubim that guarded the entrance to Eden stitched into the very fabric of the curtain guarding the entrance to the Holy of Holies. Exodus 21:36 states, "Make a curtain of blue, purple and scarlet yarn and finely twisted linen, with cherubim woven into it by a skilled worker."

Cherubim guarded the way back to life.

The medium of the temple told a story filled with longing. The palm trees carved into the walls pointed backward in time to Eden—to the tree of life now cut off. Not only did the temple forms speak a message of longing for things past, they also whispered of things still to come. The bread, the sacrifice, the curtain itself all looked forward to the one who would finally lay down his life as a final sacrifice, an act which would someday tear the curtain and restore the lost connection.

If the *medium is the message,* then the temple forms made perfect sense. The structures accurately reflected Israel's place in the story of God. Temple, priest, law and sacrifice all worked together to communicate God's faithfulness—past, present and future.

Imagine being a part of the festival procession to the temple, singing the Psalms of Ascent on the way up the mountain to Jerusalem! How glorious! If the temple is where God chooses to make his presence known, then it makes perfect sense for worship to rise on the way up to the temple. If the temple is the center of God's holiness, then religious life *should* be centered around the temple. That is where the sacrifice *should* take place. That is where the holy people *should* work.

But what about us? Should our religion be centered in a *fourth place*? Do our media accurately reflect *our* relationship to God? Hold onto those questions for just a moment.

Temple Media

As we progress through this book, we are going on a journey of church media. As we do, we will pay special attention to three categories: **place**, **people** and **practices**. These three categories will help us to analyze and evaluate changes in forms over time.

Place refers to geography and architecture. Within this category we will ask questions about land, location, buildings, materials and design.

People refers to who does what. How are humans treated in terms of hierarchy? We will ask questions about leadership. How are leaders differentiated from everyone else? What roles do they have? How are "insiders" and "outsiders" treated?

Practices refers to what we do. We will ask questions about life in community. How do people grow? What constitutes worship? What do people do when they gather? What do they do when they are apart? What are their priorities?

As we evaluate our media, we will speak of a continuum between the two extremes of **separation** and **integration**. Life rarely contains blacks and whites, so we will look for themes and patterns that give us clues as to the leanings of a particular form.

What do we observe when we look at the forms of the Jerusalem temple?

When we look at the temple system, we see a leaning toward a message of **separation**. The medium matches the message. We were separated from God, so the medium reflected this reality.

Here is what we see when we apply our three categories:

Place: The land the temple was built on was separated from the rest of Israel. Even the various courts of the temple were built out in concentric circles so as to convey the ever-increasing levels of separation. The more holy things went toward the center. On the outskirts were the less holy things. At the center stood the Holy of Holies, a place so set apart that only one priest could enter and only once a year.

People: People were separated based on family line, rank and gender. A select family line, the Levites, ran the temple. Select people from within that family line were permitted in the holiest places. The other tribes came to the temple for worship and festivals. Priests mediated between the people and God. Common people went to the priest for cleansing, prayer and forgiveness. If you were a gentile outsider or a woman, getting to the center was not an option.

Practices: Certain sacrifices, prayers, blessings and offerings were only performed by certain people and in certain places. There was a high degree of ceremony and liturgy. Music and festivals were all centered around the temple. The tithe went to support the centralized worship system of holy people and places.

When we look at Israel's temple forms, we see a consistent message. God is holy. God is set apart. From what? From things that are unholy. Remember, the word holy means *set apart* or *separate*. The forms of **place, people** and **practices** all affirm this basic message.

If I were to summarize the temple forms in one sentence, it is **a holy place where holy people do holy things**. That is the essence of a religious *fourth place*.

Now we know that Israel's relationship with God was more dynamic than just the Jerusalem temple. There was a mountain, and fire, a tabernacle and eventually the synagogue. God spoke through prophets and the Angel of the Lord and even a donkey. I am not attempting to summarize the entire Old Testament here. I am only giving a picture of one of the main forms in which Israel encountered God, the temple system.

I am focusing on the temple because it is very significant for the church in our modern era. I am making a case that the Western church is still in large part using temple media today. This is not to say there was anything wrong with the Old Testament temple. On the contrary, God himself gave the instructions for the temple. My point is not that the temple was bad. My point is that it was the correct medium **for its time**. But not for us. Not for the church of Jesus. Not for the temple of the Holy Spirit.

In Chapter 4 we are going to learn the story of Constantine. When Christianity became the official religion of Rome, Constantine wanted to present himself as a new Moses, a new David. He used an abusive version of Old Testament temple medium to impose Christianity on the world. While the Old Testament temple was a beautiful gift from God, Constantine's temple was the wrong medium for the wrong time.

In order to understand Constantine and later Christendom, we need to understand the relational reality that temple forms are designed to convey; they are designed to communicate **separation**.

That's what *fourth places* do—they separate things.

They divide insider from outsider, holy from unholy, sacred from secular. What country clubs do in the social sphere, temples do in the religious sphere. And it is the exact opposite of what Jesus came to do. He came to restore. To connect. To reconcile. To bring separated things back together.

Church Forms

I made the claim in the first chapter that most of our churches are part of the *fourth place*. Hopefully you have been asking yourself the question, "Is that true? Are we part of the *fourth place*? Are we really using temple media today?"

Let me ask the question another way—do our forms speak of **separation** or **integration**? I would suggest that most of our church forms today lean more toward **separation**.

Of course, it is rarely black or white. Clearly there are all kinds of churches and all kinds of media, especially when we consider Eastern and Western church expressions. I will state at the outset that my focus will primarily be on the West—those cultures most directly shaped by European thought and civilization.

Consider the average Western person's view of what *church* means. For most people, church is an event they go to at a religious building where professional clergy lead the people in religious practices. In terms of **place, people** and **practices**, notice how our media are very similar to those of the temple:

Place: We have separate religious buildings where we go to worship God.

People: We separate clergy from laity (everyone not a professional Christian); a professional "sacred" class distinct from "secular" occupations. People who are pastors are seen as more called to do God's work than the rest of us. The US Tax Code even validates this distinction.

Practices: We typically think of worship as the things we do at the religious building. Even if our theology tells us that worship is all of life, our church budgets, stages, staffing and Sunday anxiety all reflect worship as focused in the building.

Let's be honest, when you say the word *worship*, most people will picture a band or a choir on a stage and a room full of people singing. Many of us don't know that church can or should be any different from that. That's okay. For now, I just want to get us seriously considering the question, do our forms emphasize **separation** or **integration**? Again, I'm not referring to the sermon content or the song lyrics, just the structures.

I would argue that both our basic definition of church AND that of the temple could be summarized with the same phrase: **a holy place where holy people do holy things.** We are a religious *fourth place*. This is a problem. Why? Because the gospel speaks of radical **integration**.

No more Holy of Holies. The curtain was torn.
No more priests. We all have direct access to God.
No more sacrifices. We are already holy because of one sacrifice—Jesus.

Our forms should proclaim these great messages. They don't. They still speak messages of separation.

Of course I am not saying that all Christians only try to connect to God at their building. I am not saying everyone thinks their pastor is their only link to God or that singing is their only worship. I am not saying that we are teaching the wrong messages. I'm saying that our media are speaking their own messages. And they are loud.

The reason we so often have to remind people that worship is all of life is because our forms are speaking the opposite message. The reason people still need the senior pastor to show up when they are in the hospital is that our stages are still elevating them above the rest of us.

Regardless of what we say with our mouths, our *fourth place* media are still at work.

When people show up at a church and make a joke that God is going to strike them with lightning because of what they've done, it's because they see our buildings as a holy place. When people are afraid to use their normal colorful language around a person because he or she is a pastor, it is because they see them as a holy person. Our forms are separating us from our world.

Think about it. If our buildings are saying, "This is God's house," then what is that saying about the rest of the world? If our pulpits are saying, "This is God's man," what are they saying about the rest of us? If our music is saying, "This is God's worship," what does that mean for the rest of life?

Brick Solutions
by Dudley Callison

I was invited to preach at a church that had been in decline for fifteen years. The regional leader plotted the trajectory and determined that within twelve more years the church would close if something didn't change. When I arrived, I noticed that the front of the church was odd. A brick wall contained double doors, and behind them were the original steps and front doors of the church. I asked about this out of curiosity. A deacon explained, "We were having a terrible problem with homeless people on our steps on Sundays. So we solved the problem by adding a brick wall that prevented them from accessing our front steps. It worked!" Sadly, I asked him when this construction took place. His answer, "About fifteen years ago." I thought to myself, "Maybe your church is in decline because you designed your building to exclude the very people Jesus came to love."

People who don't believe in Jesus don't just feel judged because of what we say. They feel judged because our buildings look holier than thou. Our stages look superior to thou. Our worship is so one-dimensional that real art looks profane. Our definition of God's work is so limited that people actually start to believe that being a doctor or electrician or teacher is less holy than being a pastor.

What a tragedy to think that all of God's goodness, beauty, creativity and justice are all locked up in a dusty old building. No! The curtain was torn. The antenna was restored. All of life is worship. All of life is God's. Do we understand what our media are doing to our message?

Now this is just the tip of the iceberg. This is simply to get us warmed up. I understand that it is hard to even imagine what media pointing toward **integration** might look like.

We will discuss integration much more in the next chapter. To start though, we need to admit that yes, indeed, many of our forms speak messages of separation—clergy and laity, insiders and outsiders, sacred and secular. We are part of the *fourth place*.

Why Did It Work Before?

I understand this may be a stretch for a lot of people. This may be a pretty different paradigm for understanding church. Maybe you have some questions at this point. Why did church seem to work so well before? If this is true, then why is it just coming up now? I see what you mean about public perception of church and people feeling judged, but why did church work for my parents and grandparents? Why is it still working in the Bible belt or for more rural areas?

Those are great questions.

To help answer them, Tim Keller, Alan Roxborough, Alan Hirsch, Phyllis Tickle and many others would point to a major cultural shift happening in the West over the past century. According to Keller, "Until the middle of the 20th century...most conservative Christians in Western societies felt basically at home in their own cultures."[6] He states, "...that [earlier] era had cultural consensus about basic moral convictions."[7]

In other words, if you have a dominant Christian culture and that culture is pretty homogenous, temple forms will still do okay. That's what they were designed for. One nation. One culture. One language.

But aside from a few places, that is no longer the world in which we live. If you have wondered why Sunday morning is the most racially segregated time of the week, this is the reason. Each tribe goes to their own *fourth place*. If your church is struggling trying to figure out how to lead worship for multiple languages, multiple races, multiple economic classes, this is why. Temple forms don't cross cultures well. Temple forms are great at attracting people to one dominant religious culture. Unfortunately, they are terrible at affirming a world of diversity.

Thankfully, Jesus gave us a better way. In the next chapter we will look at how Jesus moved church *out of the fourth place* and back into the full range of life.

Sermons Not Enough

Many people will read this and think, "Wow, sounds like I need to do another sermon series on treating all of life as worship." But our problem is not a lack of preaching. Our problem is that our media are preaching their own messages and they are often out-preaching our sermons. We can teach and preach until we are out of breath, but as long as our forms are working against us, we will see limited progress for the message of Jesus.

---

[6] Tim Keller, *Center Church* (Grand Rapids: Zondervan, 2012), 181.
[7] Keller, 182.

You may be wondering why in the world we would be doing this. Where did our practices come from if not from the New Testament and Jesus? There are very good historical reasons we are doing the things we are doing. But no, our basic church media do not come from the New Testament, nor Jesus, but from several centuries after Christ.

For now, what is most important is that we face our reality: when our people think about the word *church*, they picture **a holy place where holy people do holy things**.

When Jesus said, "Destroy this temple, and I will raise it again in three days" (John 2:19), we know he was talking about his body, not about bricks. We know that when he sent the Holy Spirit in Acts, the body of believers became the "temple of the Holy Spirit" (1 Cor. 6:19). We know this to be true theologically. The temple is made of people, not buildings. Church is a community, not an event. We even say it with our mouths and with our sermons. The problem is, we deny it with our forms.

Like it or not, to our people, the church is a building. If you ask them, "Where is your church?" they will give you an address. We may have small groups, classes and other forms which modify the basic paradigm slightly, but our budgets, staffing models and people will all attest that church is primarily about **a holy place where holy people do holy things**.

That is our basic paradigm—just like the Old Testament temple. This wouldn't be such a big deal if God still lived in a building. We could all give the same address: Jerusalem, Mount Moriah, The Temple Mount. We would all know where to point.

What if God, however, were to dwell in a person? Where would we point? What address would we give? What if God himself came to earth as a baby? If the center of worship is wherever God dwells, then what if God were to eat with prostitutes? Wherever God would go, wouldn't *that* be the center of worship?

The Mobile Temple

When Jesus showed up, everything about temple media was supposed to change from stones to flesh—from centered to mobile. Jesus was a mobile man in a desktop world, a walking technological shift.

"Jesus was a mobile man in a desktop world."

Let's look at one story from his life as an example. One day Jesus happened upon a woman who had been bleeding for twelve years. Everyone avoided her. She was a pariah, a social outcast because she was unclean. The law had a rule about it found in Leviticus 15:19:

> When a woman has a discharge, and the discharge in her body is blood, she shall be in her menstrual impurity for seven days, and whoever touches her shall be unclean until the evening.

Not only did she deal everyday with the misery of her health crisis, she had to deal with the looks, the glares, the children hiding behind their parents' legs. She was unclean. Anyone who touched her would be defiled.

Then something amazing happened. This woman came right up to Jesus and touched the edge of his cloak. And guess what? Jesus was not defiled. In fact, it was just the opposite; the woman was made clean! What happened? Did Jesus not have to follow the law? Was he impervious to defilement? Every other Jew who touched this woman would have had to go back to the center, back to the temple for cleansing. What was the difference for Jesus?

The difference was the temple. Instead of the woman having to go to the temple, the temple came to her. All that the temple represented—the priest, the prophet, the sacrifice for sin, the cleansing of defilement—were at once present to this woman at the simple touch of a robe. Jesus was and is the temple.

Jesus lived *the everywhere worship of Eden*. Wherever Jesus went he was connected to his Father. And when he returned to the Father, the Holy Spirit was sent out so that now every believer would become the temple of the Holy Spirit. Every believer would now have direct access to God at all times and in all places. We would all be mobile. We would all be re-connected. The antenna would be recreated. No more need for a *fourth place*.

The *physical* temple in Jerusalem was destroyed in the year AD 70. Yet even while it stood, a fundamental shift in the temple had already taken place. The goal would no longer be about bringing people to a *fourth place* to worship God. Now worship would be about bringing the temple into the world through people full of the Holy Spirit.

The New Testament speaks of a radical integration. What was formerly broken was made right. What was formerly separated was reconciled. This message changed the world forever.

In the next chapter we're going to see what media of **integration** look like. We are going to see what happens when the medium and the message are one. Before we get there, however, I want to first let you in on some more of my own story. I want to share about my own process of being a worship leader in the church and waking up to the disturbing fact that just about everything I thought the Bible said about worship I had learned from the distorted lens of the *fourth place*.

3

Disillusioned

Many people are experiencing disillusionment when it comes to church. They know that something is wrong. They can't always name what they feel, let alone decipher how to fix it, and they are asking all kinds of questions:

Why did the early church give away money to the poor but all we seem to do is build bigger buildings?

Why do I feel like the church leaders want me to volunteer my money and time but they don't care about my life?

Why am I inspired by Jesus but Christians annoy me?

Why do I long for a safe place to process these questions but all I get from the church is platform absolutes? I want a dialogue not a monologue.

People who are experiencing disillusionment with the church use words like hypocrisy, fake, institution, organized religion, shallow, betrayal, and judgmental to describe their thoughts and feelings.

If you are feeling hurt, confused or completely done with church, you are not alone. There is nothing wrong with you. Something actually *is* wrong with the church and we need to talk about it. I am not going to pretend to have all of the answers, but I want to suggest that many of our questions are tied to the same underlying problem: we are attempting to run Christ's church from the *fourth place*. And it isn't working.

The Worship School

You might recall that after experiencing true spiritual community in college, a bunch of us moved into the same neighborhood together. During that season I was working for Russell Investments and also dedicating massive amounts of time to leading worship at a local church. Eventually, I left the world of investments and went full-time at church. Part of the job was to launch a new program called the Worship School, a seven-month internship for people who wanted to grow in their gifts as worship leaders. At the time, our worship program consisted of forty or so musicians and tech people. We wanted to train more people to support our various ministries that utilized worship personnel.

For curriculum, I had the interns read several books from successful worship ministries. I also wanted to immerse them in scripture so I had them, over the course of the seven months, read through the entire New Testament. The assignment was to write down every verse they encountered on worship in a journal. It was quite a project. Once a week we processed our findings together.

It was in this Bible study that my own feelings of disillusionment began to form a name and some clarity. Right away we started to feel like something was off. We were looking for verses to affirm our version of worship and church, but it wasn't working. We scoured the pages of the New Testament to figure out how to plan and run worship services, but what we were trying to learn simply wasn't what the New Testament was trying to teach. It wasn't just that the Bible didn't mention sound boards, microphones or stage lighting. We understood that the Bible was written in a different era of technology. No, the contradiction went much deeper than that.

I have been to numerous worship conferences and have read countless worship books. There are passages of scripture every worship leader knows by heart. As we read the New Testament together I began to realize that these familiar passages had little or nothing to do with my *fourth place* paradigm of worship services. Sometimes they even contradicted my paradigm.

For example, we studied Romans 12:1, which reads, "Offer your bodies as a living sacrifice, holy and pleasing to God—this is your true and proper worship." I can't tell you how many times I have heard the idea that "offering our bodies" is about lifting our hands or dancing or kneeling as we sing. After looking more closely at the context we realized it had nothing to do with music or singing—it was about everyone using what they had to serve the people in the community.

Ephesians 5:19 mentions songs: "Speak to one another with psalms, hymns, and spiritual songs." This Bible study taught us that "speaking" had more to do with a spiritual conversation than a worship service. It follows the verse "Do not get drunk on wine" (Eph. 5:18), not because that is good general advice, but because they were gathering around a table drinking wine and enjoying conversation! They were "speaking to one another" around a table about God's goodness from the Psalms.

Paul gives the church at Corinth some of the clearest instruction in the New Testament about what to do when gathering. He says in 1 Corinthians 14:26, "What then shall we say, brothers and sisters? When you come together, each of you has a hymn, or a word of instruction, a revelation, a tongue or an interpretation. Everything must be done so that the church may be built up."

Paul's description is of a community where everyone participates. There are no consumers, no observers; there are no performers. The believers did not contrive an environment of lights, smoke and professional talent. They weren't striving after trendy, cool, hipster, ancient or new. They simply brought who they were and what they had and offered it to God and to each other.

Our internship was focused on creating *excellent* worship, but we didn't see anything in the New Testament that looked remotely like our definition of excellence.

Acts 13:2 talks about Paul and others "worshipping the Lord and fasting," but even the Greek word for *worship* in verses like this is more properly translated as *ministering* or *serving*. That's not to say that they never sang, but there is universal agreement among scholars that the church did not even allow musical instruments for the first 400 years![8] They certainly sang. They certainly communed with the Lord together; however, what they called *ministering to the Lord* was more of a blend of corporate prayer, hymns, spiritual gifts and scripture reading. The point was that everyone brought something to the table, not to the stage.

Worship pastors, one of the first and most vital hires for modern church plants, aren't even mentioned in the New Testament. We have to go to Old Testament temple passages to find anything remotely similar.
I love music. I have recorded albums and been in a band. Looking through the New Testament to find what we do on Sunday mornings is a lost cause. Go to the Psalms. Go to Old Testament temple passages. Maybe go to heaven in Revelation, but even there, you're in the heavenly throne room, not the New Testament church.

---

[8] Joseph A. Jungmann. Trans by Francis A. Brunner, *The Early Liturgy: To the Time of Gregory the Great* (Notre Dame: University of Notre Dame Press, 1959), 124.

My disillusionment started to spread well beyond worship leading. I started asking questions about sermons and tithing and buildings. I read everything I could get my hands on. Old books. Modern books. My disillusionment only grew. I went through bouts of bitterness, anger and confusion. Eventually, I spent three years at Denver Seminary to study these questions.

Now with years of experiences like these behind me, it's no longer disillusionment for me. I have clarity. I believe at the core of my being that the modern church is attempting to live out a gospel of radical **integration** on a foundation of **separation**. We are preaching an incarnate Christ from a platform removed from culture. We are telling the story of a suffering servant from a celebrity stage. The medium and the message are at odds.

Church is in the wrong place, the *fourth place*. Our people are getting mixed messages.

So what do we do about it?

The Media of Integration

If we want to move from a place of disillusionment to clarity, the first step is understanding the New Testament on its own terms. Rather than reading the Bible through the interpretive lens of the *fourth place*, let's look at the New Testament through the lens of **integration**.

When we were reconciled to God, the broken antenna was restored. We no longer required a *particular* place. The temple was free to leave the building.

Let's again utilize our media of **place, people,** and **practices** to see how the New Testament reflected this new reality in Christ.

Place

The New Testament is the story of the temple moving into culture.

The followers of Jesus had no central building. Instead, one of the primary ways that they self-identified was as strangers scattered throughout the world. They were exiles—a people with a home in heaven, but nowhere to call home on earth.

They did church here:

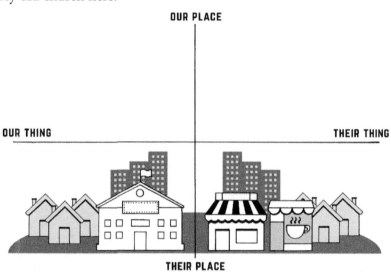

Note: The modern buildings help us imagine this for ourselves.

The early church gathered wherever they could best integrate with culture. While the home, the *first place*, was one of their primary gathering places, they met in any type of location that made sense for their purposes and size. Public spaces, work, prisons, the marketplace, river beds, catacombs and mountains all became places for the church to gather.[9] In Acts 2, we see the church gathering in the *temple courts*.

[9] Edward Adams, *The Earliest Christian Meeting Places* (New York: Bloomsbury, 2013).

While this may sound like a religious place, Solomon's Colonnade, where they met, was actually a public place in the outer courts full of all types of people and business—a *second* and *third place*.

Now some might ask, "Isn't the main reason they met in those places because of persecution? If they had the opportunity, resources, and size, wouldn't they have designed buildings like us?" Great question, but no. The reasons for the lack of buildings were not merely passive. In fact, the evidence shows that the early church *actively* resisted the creation of religious buildings.

The end of religious architecture was actually a core part of their ecclesiology—their beliefs about how church should work. Paul repeatedly told the people that they were the building (1 Cor. 3:9, 3:16, 6:19, 2 Cor. 6:16, Eph. 2:21-22). Peter told the people that they were the building (1 Pet. 2:5). This was a radical concept for good, observant Jews whose way of life and culture revolved around a physical temple. Something monumental must have happened for them to believe the temple had moved into a community of people.

Municius Felix, an early church father writing around the turn of the second century, wrote:

> But do you think that we conceal what we worship, if we have not temples and altars? And yet what image of God shall I make, since, if you think rightly, man himself is the image of God? What temple shall I build to Him, when this whole world fashioned by His work cannot receive Him? And when I, a man, dwell far and wide, shall I shut up the might of so great majesty within one little building?[10]

---

[10] "The Octavius of Municius Felix," Chap. xxxii, trans. by Robert Ernest Wallis, PhD. in *The Ante-Nicene Fathers* Vol iv (Buffalo, NY: The Christian Literature Company, 1885), 193.

Tertullian, a contemporary of Felix, wrote similar sentiments when writing to Roman leaders about the Christians:

> We have filled every place among you—cities, islands, fortresses, towns, market-places, the very camp, tribes, companies, palace, senate, forum,—we have left nothing to you but the temples of your gods.[11]

We left you only the temples. Christians were intentionally staying away from religious buildings and instead putting themselves into every other sphere of culture. It wasn't that they couldn't afford buildings or hadn't thought up the concept yet; rather, they were consciously working to **integrate** with culture and avoid being like the other religions. They didn't *want* temples. They didn't want a *fourth place*.

As much as the temple was based on **separation**, the church was based on **integration**. They were following Jesus, the one who incarnated himself into the world, the one without a home, the one who ate and lived among sinners.

Now, I understand that for many of us, trying to imagine church without buildings is a real stretch. If you are starting from a position where you already own a building, we will discuss wonderful possibilities to practice **integration** utilizing your existing facility. For now, I just want us to look at the forms of the early church. Let's allow the early church to speak for itself without all of the modern assumptions about church architecture.

Some may also be wondering about the Jewish synagogue as a gathering place. Clearly Jesus spent regular time in the synagogue as did Paul on

---

[11] Tertullian, "The Apology" xxxvii, trans. by The Rev. S. Thelwall in *The Ante-Nicene Fathers* Vol iii, *Latin Christianity: Its Founder, Tertullian* (Buffalo, NY: The Christian Literature Company, 1885) 45.

his missionary journeys. However, as the church spread, we see no evidence of the church constructing anything new resembling the synagogue. In other words, Jesus spent time there because Jesus was a Jew, not because of the new mission. Paul spent time there in order to preach the gospel to Jews, but it had more to do with incarnating the gospel into existing Jewish culture than adopting a building style that would be repeated by the early church. As the faith spread, they did not build synagogues, but integrated themselves into the world in which they lived.

Tertullian's list says Christians integrated with every sphere of culture—political, military, economic, judicial, the work places, the cities. Everywhere people lived, died, did business, played, governed and more—that's where the Christians went. That's what it means for the church to be **incarnational**—to live and gather among the culture following the pattern of Jesus.

For the first two hundred years of Christianity there was no interest in constructing religious buildings, only integrating the kingdom into what already existed. Jesus says in Luke 13:20-21, "What shall I compare the kingdom of God to? It is like yeast that a woman took and mixed into about sixty pounds of flour until it worked all through the dough." Sixty pounds! That's a lot of dough! Why so much? Because the world is a big place and every culture, language, subculture, home, farm and prison needs to be filled with the kingdom of God.

A Change in Function

Jesus' coming meant a **functional** change for the temple. I will unpack this in detail in Chapter 8, and I want to bring it up here as well. In design theory, **form** is supposed to follow **function**. This means that our purpose, our function, should drive our forms. The Old Testament temple performed a certain function. God wanted to use Israel as a light to the nations. The *physical* temple drew people toward the center and toward that light. However, something remarkable happened in

Christ—the light went mobile. There was a functional change. The function was no longer, *get the world to the light*, but instead *get the light to the world*.

God has always been a sending God. The temple has always been for all nations. Now that the relationship had been restored, it was time for a new medium—one that could go *to* the nations, rather than expecting the nations to come to it.

How do you spread the light into every culture, every tribe, and every language without destroying their beautiful diversity? You make the temple out of people. After all, what do all cultures have in common? Certainly not architecture. Buildings are culturally bound. If the early church would have built Jewish synagogues their mission would have stalled-out in Israel. But if you make the temple out of people, then you have a vehicle that can carry the light to the entire world. If you make your central gathering a meal, then you have something every culture can understand and do together. There was a change in function, and that function required a new form—a human temple.

It was not an accident that the early Christians avoided their own buildings. A movement started by a carpenter certainly could have involved construction projects.

It wasn't that Christians in the early church were unaware of large buildings. To the contrary, they were surrounded by Roman temples, coliseums and basilica. It wasn't that all Christians were poor and persecuted. There were plenty of seasons of Christian freedom from persecution. Paul was a Roman citizen and could have easily gone on his church fund-raising journey to raise money for a building project in Corinth instead of supporting people dying of a Jerusalem famine. He didn't. Why not? Because he wanted to restore human temples dying of starvation, not physical temples dying for a remodel.

The early church carried an ethos of **integration** with culture, not **separation** from culture. Paul had no interest in attracting people to a polished event in a beautiful building. The early church was not trying to get people into their Christian temples, they were trying to get the living temple into their world.

Next Generation
by Dudley Callison

We gathered a bunch of leaders of the next generation and asked them, "What will church look like for you in the future?" Their answers were inspirational. None of their answers was rooted in buildings, staff or programs. Millennials don't care so much about denominations, nor do they intend to join a church and spend their money on keeping the doors open. In fact, they categorically see the church as poor stewards of resources that could be used to solve global issues. They want meaningful community, creative interaction with God, and behaviors that meet real-time human needs. In Communitas we envision "churches that think, care and act like Jesus in our world."

People

Just as the temple change meant a radical departure from a physical **place**, it also meant a radical leveling of the priesthood. Before, only certain people of a certain gender in a certain tribe were able to perform the religious duties. Jesus was the great leveler. He put religious leaders on the same level as prostitutes. All people, all races, male and female, Jew and Gentile, slave and free, could all participate in the church. Everyone was an important part of the body.

Why? Because the curtain was torn in two. They no longer needed to access God through a priest. Now everyone had access to the Spirit.

Everyone was a priest. Everyone had something to give. If everyone is full of God, why should one senior priest do all of the work?

In the early church, team leadership was the norm. A group of elders was formed to help oversee each church community. Deacons helped serve. The basic rule was participation; everyone played a role. There were clearly leaders present with specific duties, but they led from *within* the community as servants, not *up front* or separate from the community.

If you are a ministry professional or earn your paycheck from the church, stay with me. Saying that we need mutual participation in the church in no way indicates a lack of organization or structure. No, the early church still needed strong leadership. Though not centered in offices in religious buildings, they still had an intricate relational network requiring full-time care. We will cover this in depth in Chapters 6 and 10. For now, just observe some of the ways the early church promoted a spirit of mutual participation.

As you read this description from Tertullian of an early church gathering, try NOT to imagine your church building. Try to imagine instead the third floor of a home in an open, lamplit dining room similar to that of the last supper.

> The nature of our meal and its purpose are explained by its very name. It is called *Agape*, as the Greeks call love in its purest sense. However much it may cost, it is always a gain to be extravagant in the name of fellowship with what is God's, since the food brought is used for the benefit of all who are in need. To respect the lowly is all-important with God.
>
> ...The participants do not go to the table unless they have first tasted of prayer to God. As much is eaten as is necessary to satisfy the hungry; as much is drunk as is good for those who live a disciplined life. When satisfying themselves they

are aware that even during the night they should worship God. They converse as those who are aware that God is listening.

After the hands are washed and the lights are lit, all are asked to stand forth and to praise God as well as each is able, be it from the holy scriptures or from their own heart. From this it will be recognized "how he drank." In like manner the meal is closed with a prayer. After this we part from one another…always pursuing the same self-control and purity as befits those who have taken in a truth rather than a meal. This is the way Christians meet.[12]

How does Tertullian's gathering compare to your typical church service? What is the same? What is different?

When I read this, I can't help but want to be a part of that kind of gathering! It sounds life giving and relaxed. Believers get to hang out together, drink wine, eat a good meal, love the poor, hear from each other and pray together. It sounds like spiritual family, not spiritual performance.

Some reading this may think, "That sounds more like my small group than my church service." Good observation. Remember though, when Tertullian says, "This is the way Christians meet," he is implying that this meal was their primary gathering, not an optional add-on like many of our modern small groups.

When Jesus came as the Great High Priest he changed the definition of the temple. Church was not an event to be attended, but a community of love and acceptance. The church did not connect to God through one holy priest, but instead found Christ in each other.

---

12 Tertullian, "Apology," xxxix, in Eberhard Arnold, *The Early Christians in Their Own Words* (Farmington, PA: Plough Publishing House, 1998), 246-247.

Church was not a holy place where holy people did holy things, but a spiritual family.

Practices

There is a reason all religions of the world use temple forms. They communicate distance between the holy and the unholy. They create dependency because they communicate a lack.

> *You lack knowledge. Come to the guru.*
> *You lack health. Come to the temple for healing.*
> *You are unclean. Come and wash.*
> *You have sinned. Come and sacrifice.*

Once again, Jesus' life, death and resurrection marked a functional change for the temple. Jesus was the final sacrifice. All believers in Christ were made clean. All believers were forgiven. There was no longer a lack. Now, instead of bringing needy people to the temple, we could bring the temple to the needs of the world. We don't do this because we have it all together or have all of the answers, but because we carry in our weak and frail "jars of clay" the living God (2 Cor. 4:7).

Everything the temple represented is now embodied in a community of believers.

That's why the temple language we *do* encounter in the New Testament is always radically re-interpreted to talk about people. Paul, for example, borrows the temple language of a *drink offering* to talk about the end of his life and ministry. "For I am already being poured out like a drink offering, and the time for my departure is near" (2 Tim. 4:6). Paul says in Romans 12:1, "Offer your bodies as living sacrifices, holy and pleasing to God—this is your true and proper worship." Again, the language of temple sacrifice is borrowed to talk about the commitment to each other in the body.

Where is the sacrifice? Where is worship? In a building? No, it is anywhere, everywhere, the followers of Jesus offer their lives for each other and for their communities.

The writer of Hebrews explains this shift. If you are new to Hebrews or the language of the Old Testament sacrificial system, this passage could be a bit confusing. The writer here is saying that worship used to take place on a physical altar—the place where they did the sacrifices in the temple. He refers to this as *inside the camp*. *Camp* here refers to the Jewish tabernacle—the predecessor to the temple. People had to go *inside the camp* to get to the holy places and perform their sacrifices. In Hebrews 13:9-16, the writer explains how all of this changed through Jesus:

> Do not be carried away by all kinds of strange teachings. It is good for our hearts to be strengthened by grace, not by eating ceremonial foods, which is of no benefit to those who do so. We have an altar from which those who minister at the tabernacle have no right to eat. The high priest carries the blood of animals into the Most Holy Place as a sin offering, but the bodies are burned outside the camp. And so Jesus also suffered outside the city gate to make the people holy through his own blood. Let us, then, go to him outside the camp, bearing the disgrace he bore. For here we do not have an enduring city, but we are looking for the city that is to come. Through Jesus, therefore, let us continually offer to God a sacrifice of praise—the fruit of lips that openly profess his name. And do not forget to do good and to share with others, for with such sacrifices God is pleased.

Where is the altar? In front of the worship center or sanctuary? No, the altar is not in the temple and it is not in your church building. The *world* is the altar! What is the sacrifice? An animal? People singing at church? No, the sacrifice is real people offering their lives for others. It is people living like Jesus by doing good and sharing with others.

Do you know what happened *outside the camp* in the Old Testament? Outside the camp was where they isolated diseased people (Lev. 13:46). Outside the camp was where the people went with a shovel to relieve themselves (Deut. 23:12-13).

Guess where our altar is? Outside the camp. Guess where we are to be a living sacrifice? Outside the camp. Outside the religious system. Out in the mess of culture. There is no inside or outside anymore! This new reality has massive implications on church practices, especially our worship.

Jesus' coming marked an end to a central altar and a return to *the everywhere worship of Eden*. The integration of our **practices** meant a return to all of life as worship.

Now don't get me wrong. I like a lot of our worship songs. Some are catchy. Most contain beautiful truths. Unfortunately, many of them take something that was supposed to happen outside the *fourth place* and they put it right back on the stage. Consider the lyrics to a well-known worship song:

> "We bring a sacrifice of praise
> Into the house of the Lord."[13]

Some of you probably know this song. I grew up singing it. It's a good song and I'm sure it was written with a good heart. But do you see the tension? Hebrews 13:15-16 tells us that a "sacrifice of praise" is "to do good and to share with those in need." Where? Outside the religious zone—out there in the streets and alleys and neighborhoods. That's what the early church actually believed and practiced. Municius Felix described this when he wrote,

---

[13] Kirk Deadman, "We Bring a Sacrifice of Praise," John T. Benson Publishing Co., 1984.

He who cultivates justice makes offerings to God; he who abstains from fraudulent practices propitiates God; he who snatches man from danger slaughters the most acceptable victim. These are our sacrifices, these are our rites of God's worship; thus, among us, he who is most just is he who is most religious.[14]

Jesus integrated **place, people** and **practices**. When the temple moved into culture, every part of our lives as his followers was supposed to follow suit.

To summarize where we have come so far, the following table is helpful:

	PHYSICAL TEMPLE	JESUS AS THE TEMPLE	CHURCH AS THE TEMPLE
PLACE—LOCATION	JERUSALEM	JESUS' BODY	COMMUNITY OF BELIEVERS
PEOPLE—LEADERSHIP	SELECT PRIESTS	JESUS THE HIGH PRIEST	COMMUNITY OF PRIESTS
PRACTICES—WORSHIP	SACRIFICIAL SYSTEM	JESUS THE FINAL SACRIFICE	LIVING SACRIFICES FOR EACH OTHER

The Bible communicates a movement from a physical temple, to Jesus as the temple, and finally to the church, a community, as the temple. This is not some strange new dispensationalism; this is what the Bible teaches.

A New Wineskin

It has taken a long time to realize how I was reading the Bible through the wrong lens. Paradigm shifts can feel unsettling and quite painful. When Jesus spoke of this type of change, he used the image of a wineskin. He said that new wine will cause old wineskins to break.

---

[14] Felix, *The Ante-Nicene Fathers* Vol. iv, 193.

I have been there. As our worship interns and I read through the New Testament, it sent me on a bit of a tailspin. Just as Jesus promised, my wineskin was starting to crack. My old assumptions simply could not contain the new wine.

If your wineskins are starting to crack, it's okay. It's good, in fact. Take your time. Read a lot of books. Ask great questions. Discuss this with friends. When I began to understand this new wineskin of church and worship, the entire New Testament started opening up to me. It started to make sense why there are so few mentions of the word worship, or singing, or tithing, or anything resembling excellent performance. At the same time it started to make sense why there are abundant instructions about how to live in community. If the new worship is sacrificial living for each other, then there are all kinds of instructions about worship! Love one another. Encourage one another. Serve one another. The list goes on and on.[15]

A Misunderstood Woman

Earlier in the chapter I shared several passages that I had formerly misread under my *fourth place* lens. I saved the best for last. It is the story of the woman at the well.

If there is any passage known to all worship leaders it is the phrase about "worship in Spirit and truth." I can't tell you how many times I have heard it taught or preached that "Spirit and truth" means that our worship services should be a good balance of both emotion and biblical truth—or in more charismatic circles, "Spirit and truth" is about the balance of spiritual gifts and Biblical doctrine. Either way, it is regularly

---

[15] Scholar Andrew B. McGowan writes, "'Worship' language in the NT texts suggests a great deal about ethos or a Christian way of life, but relatively little about the specifics of distinctive liturgical practice or performance." Andrew B. McGowan, *Ancient Christian Worship* (Grand Rapids, MI: Baker Academic, 2014), 7.

taught that "worship in Spirit and truth" is all about worship services and how to keep them balanced.

I want to close this chapter at the well of Sychar because this amazingly misunderstood woman represents the whole point of this book. Many people interpret this story to be about worship services when ironically the point is actually quite the opposite.

I don't know how you have heard it taught in the past. There are quite a few regular sermons preached on John 4. One focuses on the first part, that Jesus decided to go through Sychar, the despised Samaritan town, instead of going around Samaria like most good observant Jews. It is a story about crossing cultures. Another is the angle of being born again and receiving the living water. Yet another is the woman's checkered sexual past and Jesus' love for her.

Normally when we get to the part about "worship in Spirit and truth," we treat this like it's a tangent. We say that she wanted to change the subject. She didn't want to talk about her sexual brokenness, her relational disappointment, her community exclusion, her shame, so she brings up worship. We then go on to imagine that "worship in Spirit and truth" is about balanced worship services.

Does that make any sense? A hurting, shame-filled woman asks a question about which temple to worship at, the Samaritan one at Mount Gerazim, or the Jewish one in Jerusalem, and Jesus decides to lecture her about balanced worship services? I don't think so.

This woman and her people have a very real question about legitimate worship. To them, the temple was the only place of true worship. If you went to the wrong place, your worship didn't count. So where was the right place? Where did God dwell? The Samaritans said is was Mount Gerazim in Samaria. The Jews said it was Mount Moriah, The Temple Mount, in Jerusalem. Who was right?

For centuries this Samaritan woman's people had been despised by the Jews. The Jews had even destroyed the Samaritan temple in 128 BC.[16] Now, finally, sitting in front of her was someone who might actually answer for God on behalf of the truth, a real prophet. If he knew the truth of her marital history, maybe he could answer the deepest question of her people. This is not a random tangent.

She asks about the true place to worship. Her paradigm is revealed in her question. She was asking a question from the paradigm of *physical* temple worship—*fourth place* worship. We are very similar to this woman. We continue today to ask the same types of questions: What is the right way to worship? With drums? With liturgy? With hymns? With smoke machines?

Jesus' response is remarkable. He blows up her paradigm (and our paradigm) and reveals a new wineskin of church and worship that she never could have possibly conceived—a wineskin based not on religious centers of worship but on people born of the Spirit.

We have to go back a chapter in John to understand the extent of what is happening here. In John 3, Jesus had a conversation with a man named Nicodemus. Nicodemus was a respected Jewish leader who snuck over to Jesus under the cover of night. Nicodemus represents the religious elite, the insiders. Jesus tells Nicodemus about the Holy Spirit, about being born again. Nicodemus doesn't get it.

Then, in John 4, Jesus gives a Holy Spirit lesson to someone on the other end of the social spectrum, a despised Samaritan female outcast. This woman represents the hated outsiders, the religious rejects. He talks to her about the Spirit as living water.

She doesn't get it either.

---

[16] Andreas J. Köstenberger, *John* (Grand Rapids: Baker Academic, 2004), 141.

Jesus is trying to tell them both that the temple paradigm is shifting from centered to mobile. Instead of brick and mortar, the temple will be people full of the Holy Spirit. *You must be born again. You must drink the living water.* Jesus tells her, "Yet a time is coming and has now come when the true worshipers will worship the Father in the Spirit and truth, for they are the kind of worshipers the Father seeks. God is spirit, and his worshipers must worship in the Spirit and in truth" (John 4:23-24).

I imagine Jesus saying it this way: *The temple used to be a place where you went to meet with God. The question of where to go to worship really mattered. You did in fact need to go to the right physical temple. But right now, sitting in front of you, I am currently the temple. I am the high priest. I am the sacrifice. And soon, when I return to the Father, you are about to be the temple.*

The point of both Nicodemus and the woman at the well, when combined, shows that the new temple paradigm applies to *all* people—the entire spectrum of humanity. The Holy of Holies is not going to be just for one special male Levite. God's presence is going to be for everyone. It's going to be for the religious elite. It's going to be for the Samaritan outcast. It's going to be about *all* people, *all* types, born of the Spirit, fully pleasing to God the Father who is NOT searching the world for properly balanced religious worship services, but for people full of his Son through the Spirit. Those are the true worshippers. This is the new paradigm.

Jesus takes the most despised human a Jew could imagine and explains to her that the center of worship is now mobile. A technology change has occurred. What used to be about a physical center of worship is now about a community of hearts on fire.

If the new paradigm of worship is no longer about **a holy place where holy people do holy things**, then how fitting is it that one of the first people to know would be the most unholy person in the most unholy place whose life has been riddled with unholy sexual practices? I love it! This rejected woman is just the type of person God wants to use to change the world.

It's a new wineskin. A temple is coming that is not built to draw people to a religious center, but to integrate the kingdom of God into every culture of the world. The church would no longer **separate**; the church would **integrate**. And that is just what happened. For nearly three hundred years, anyway.

Then along came Constantine.

4

Constantine the Architect

In 2016, the Academy Award for Best Picture went to the film *Spotlight*. In the movie, a team of journalists uncover the Catholic Church's prolonged and horrific sexual abuse cover-up in the city of Boston. In a haunting monologue, a now grown-up survivor of the abuse explains what happened to him:

> When you are a poor kid from a poor family, religion counts for a lot and when a priest pays attention to you it's a big deal. He asks you to collect the hymnals or take out the trash, you feel special. It's like God asking for help. So maybe it's a little weird when he tells you a dirty joke but now you got a secret together, so you go along. Then he shows you a porno mag and you go along, and you go along, and you go along, until one day he asks you [for sexual favors] and so you go along with that too... How do you say no to God, right?[17]

How did this happen?

---

[17] *Spotlight*, directed by Tom McCarthy, Open Road Films, 2015.

Let's not pretend that this is simply a Catholic issue. Spiritual and sexual abuse are well known in Protestant circles as well. This is not a question of Catholic or Protestant. It is a question of power. "How do you say no to God, right?"

Maybe you have similar questions:

How in the world did a movement that started in a humble manger end up in the marble halls of St. Peter's Basilica with power over the known world?

How did the Prince of Peace spread Christianity through violence?

How did evangelicals in America become enmeshed with political power?

How did we end up with Spotlight*?*

This chapter is dedicated to answering those questions.

The key antagonist in this part of the story is Emperor Constantine, though as we will see he was certainly not alone in the project. I also want to be clear that it is best to avoid two common errors when speaking of Constantine. One is to overemphasize discontinuity with the past. Some would say that prior to Constantine, Christianity was all about spontaneity and freedom, and after his reign the church suddenly became liturgical. No, the church always has and always will utilize liturgy. Liturgy itself is not the problem—rather, it is the use of liturgy for power and control that is the issue. The other common error with Constantine is to overemphasize continuity, as if Roman Catholicism was just the natural result of what Jesus began.

No, as we will see, in Constantine there is both continuity with the past and discontinuity. Much looked similar and yet something historically monumental occurred.

As we trace the development in church forms through the fourth century, you will see the medium of **integration** slowly shift back to the medium of **separation**.

If you are feeling disillusioned with the church or want to know why we do the things we do in today's church, there is a good chance your answers are deeply rooted to this era. I want to help you connect the dots. Getting church out of the *fourth place* will involve untangling ourselves from the *fourth century*. When Constantine reconstructed Christianity, he rebuilt the church on a new foundation. We need to understand that foundation if we want to excavate and eventually rebuild church on the older and better foundation of Jesus.

The Earliest Gatherings

In the first two centuries, as we have discussed, the church met primarily in public and in homes. There were no basilicas. No temples. No megachurches. We see it throughout the New Testament:

"Day after day, in the temple courts and from house to house, they never stopped teaching and proclaiming the good news that Jesus is the Christ" (Acts 5:42).

"Greet also the church that meets at their house" (Romans 16:5).

"Give my greetings to the brothers and sisters at Laodicea, and to Nympha and the church in her house" (Colossians 4:15).

We saw a snapshot of their gatherings in the previous chapter found in the writings of Tertullian. The early believers did not have the slightest interest in developing their own church architecture.

In the first half of the third century, the number of Christians increased rapidly, yet the church continued to gather in humble, nonreligious spaces. Churches converted larger homes into what they called *community centers* or *meeting houses.*[18] These would have been recognized from the street as normal residences, but the interior was altered for the specific needs of the community. They built baptisteries, a meeting room that could fit a small crowd, and storage rooms for clothing and food for the poor. A police record from *The Great Persecution* of 303 AD under Emperor Diocletian records the ransacking of one of these *community centers*. During the raid they found lamps in the meeting room, bookcases in a small library, and jugs and chests in the dining room.[19] In a storage room used for charity they confiscated eighty-two women's tunics, thirty-eight cloaks, and sixty pairs of shoes.[20] Even from a police record from 303 AD we can sense the priorities of the early church. They utilized their gathering places to incarnate themselves into their cities, serving the physical needs of their neighbors.

We see here the integration of **place, people** and **practices**. The community gathered within culture, not separate from it. Leaders led from within the community, not from a stage. Worship was holistic— yes, they had a liturgical life, but it centered around a meal in the neighborhood. Their lives were a *living sacrifice* of love for their world.

The early third century included long periods free from persecution, even times of political favor. Churches could own property, bury their dead, baptize and meet in the open. Regardless, they continued to meet in smaller spaces and their buildings did not stand out in any significant way from any of the surrounding Roman architecture.[21] In other words, even though they had greater numbers, greater resources, and lived with significant choice of location, they remained intentionally integrated into the normal fabric of culture.

---

[18] Richard Krautheimer, *Early Christian and Byzantine Architecture* (Middlesex England: Penguin Book Ltd, 1965), 27.
[19] Krautheimer, *Early Christian and Byzantine Architecture*, 31.
[20] Jungmann, *The Early Liturgy*, 16.
[21] Krautheimer, *Early Christian and Byzantine Architecture*, 26.

Seeds of Separation

Toward the end of the third century, the ethic of integration started to shift. Christians started to construct bigger buildings of their own. Not coincidentally, at the same time we also see the rise of bigger egos. For example, in 265 AD, Paul of Samosate, the bishop of Antioch, "against the wishes of his brethren," sought personal quarters more fitting a "Roman ranking magistrate" as well as applause when entering the meeting room.[22] Complaints started to rise, even from pagans, that Christian meeting places were getting more pretentious and were starting to resemble Roman temples. We see the same type of response today as many people look with disdain at those who preach a homeless Jesus, yet spend millions on their own facilities.

Eusebius, an early church historian writing in 324 AD, described the last decades of the third century. He documented the growing political power of the church rulers: "not content with the ancient buildings, they erected spacious churches...daily increasing in magnitude and improvement."[23] The buildings were growing and so was the division. Eusebius, grieving the animosity between Christians over the new buildings and growing competition in the church, recounted, "...one envying and reviling another in different ways; we were almost at the point of taking up arms against each other, assailing each other with darts as with spears."[24]

In part as a response to the Christian division caused by these new building projects, in 303 AD Roman Emperor Diocletian interrupted the period of relative peace in the church and ordered the destruction of all Christian buildings, scriptures and leaders. The Great Persecution

---

[22] Krautheimer, 37-38.
[23] Eusebius, trans. by C.F. Cruse, *Eusebius' Ecclesiastical History* (Peabody: Hendrickson Publishers, 1998), 279-80.
[24] Eusebius, 280.

broke out across the empire. Literally thousands died for their faith, including countless Christian leaders.

Constantine

In the middle of this chaos, Constantine stepped onto the stage. He was proclaimed Caesar in 306 AD. In 313 AD the "Edict of Milan"[25] was issued, which stopped all persecution and granted Christians a favored status within the empire. Finally, victory for the Christians, right? Not so much...

There is ongoing debate as to Constantine's motives. Some say he had a legitimate conversion experience and did what he thought was in the best interest of Christ's church. Others argue that he was using the Christians to gain his own control and power over a badly divided Empire. I believe the evidence shows a more complicated story. Constantine, following the tradition of Roman emperors, saw an advantage in adopting the Christian God as his patron God. He claimed Christianity as his new religion, but clearly had no intention of bowing his royal knee to what he perceived as a weak and pathetic Christ. Rather, he, in effect, removed Christ from Christianity and set himself up in Christ's place as a new messianic figure, a new Moses, ready to conquer his enemies as God conquered the peoples of the promised land. He saw himself as the savior of both Christianity and Rome—the strong Messiah the people had been waiting for.

Consider the words of Constantine's personal historian. Notice the connection he makes between Constantine and the deliverer, Moses:

---

[25] The "Edict of Milan," though formerly attributed to Constantine should probably be called "The Edict of Nicomedia." It was written by Licinius, Constantine's one-time co-emperor and ruler of the Eastern provinces. In the letter, Licinius summarizes a conversation that occurred with Constantine in Milan. David Potter, *Constantine the Emperor* (New York: Oxford University Press, 2013), 148-149.

...after the example of his great servant Moses, Constantine entered the imperial city in triumph. And here the whole body of the senate, and others of rank and distinction in the city, freed as it were from the restraint of a prison, along with the whole Roman populace, their countenances expressive of the gladness of their hearts, received his with acclamations and abounding joy; men, women, and children, with countless multitudes of servants, greeting him as deliverer, preserver, and benefactor, with incessant shouts.[26]

Moses started his deliverance after an encounter with a burning bush. Constantine started his Christian campaign claiming a vision of a cross in the sky along with the words, "in this sign, conquer." When Constantine's enemies drowned in the Tiber River, he compared it to Pharaoh's armies drowning in the Red Sea. Like Moses, Constantine even built himself a mini-tabernacle where he would go to "meet with God."[27]

Scholar Alistair Kee compares the differences between Constantine and Jesus:

If truth be told, which one looks more like a Messiah? Is it Constantine, born to the purple, who wears his rich robes easily as one who has never doubted his right to them? Or is it the son of the carpenter who, while being tortured and used for sport by the soldiers after his arrest, was made to wear a royal robe because it was so incongruous? Who looks more the part of the king who fulfills the longing for a successor to David? Surely it is the emperor in his court, surrounded by the evidences of wealth, rather than the one who can only say,

---

[26] Philip Schaff and Henry Wace, Editors, *A Select Library of Nicene and Post-Nicene Fathers of the Christian Church* (Grand Rapids: Eerdmans, 1982), 493.

[27] Alistair Kee, *Constantine Versus Christ: The Triumph of Ideology* (London: SCM Press Ltd., 1982), 119.

'Foxes have holes, and birds of the air have nests; but the son of man has nowhere to lay his head.'[28]

Did Rome become a Christian state? No, Rome was not conquered by Christ. Christ was pushed aside by Constantine. In a move of political genius he was able to do what no Roman emperor had ever done—win the Christians to his side, all the while undermining everything Christ embodied.

Much blame has been placed on Constantine for ruining Christianity. I will put a lot of blame on him as well; however, it is not as simple as pointing a finger at one man. There is plenty of evidence to show that Constantine was sincerely trying to help the church. From his legislation benefiting oppressed people groups, to his attempts to bring church unity through Nicea and other councils, his motives may have been just as pure as any one of us who tries to help Jesus along through our own systems of power.[29]

Constantine was certainly not the only one who wanted to see a state-empowered church. The seeds of "lording it over" others were already sprouting during the latter half of the third century, prior to Constantine. Christians wanted fame. They wanted power. They wanted bigger buildings. They wanted to impress people. Constantine did not act alone. Constantine had a ripe audience for his "bigger and more glorious Christianity" program. Many Christians were moving in this direction anyway. Constantine just put the royal stamp on it and all the resources of the Empire behind it.

After all, who wouldn't want a little redemption? Emperor Diocletian had just recently persecuted and executed their friends, their leaders. Who wouldn't want a reprieve from the violence? What leader doesn't

---

[28] Kee, 124.
[29] Potter, *Constantine the Emperor*, 298.

want a little public notoriety? A better paycheck? Let's be honest, Christianity wasn't free from hubris in the first two centuries either. The same lust for significance was in the apostles the night of the last supper when they argued about who was the greatest (Luke 22:24). The reality is that the same seed of pride lives in all of us. If you understand modern history, you will realize that this is not the first time nor the last time that Jesus is hijacked for political means. We will look at Constantine and his disastrous effects on Christianity, and as we do, let us also look at our own hearts. Look at your own church experience and ask yourself if the spirit of Constantine isn't alive and well today.

Whatever Constantine's motives were, what scholars agree on is that a fundamental change happened. How much of the change was directed by Constantine himself? We don't know all the details. What we do know is that under his leadership, Christianity was converted to Rome. *Christendom* was born—the rule of the Christian state. Constantine marked the marriage of political and spiritual power brokers, an unholy matrimony.

Keys to the Kingdom
by Dudley Callison

We had the joy of living in Turkey on mission for two years. Istanbul, formerly Constantinople, was the epicenter of Christendom for one thousand years. And the Hagia Sophia church was the heartbeat of the empire. After 1400 AD, it became the center of the Ottoman Empire, serving as a template for mosques built all around the world. It still stands today as a museum for both Christians and Muslims. Inside, the plaster put up by the Muslims is falling off, revealing the most amazing tile mosaic artwork which originally covered the walls. Millions of tiny tiles, all hand placed, form images of Christ and the early church. One mosaic stands out as most telling. It is a scene of the Pope and the Emperor. The Pope is handing the keys to the Kingdom of God to Constantine. In return, Constantine is giving the keys to the city to the Pope. It depicts the "wedding" of church and state—the co-mingling of power. Many have described this as the crowning achievement of the church, the moment the church was freed from state-led persecution. Looking back, we have to ask what happened to the vibrant, organic version of church that grew immensely in spite of the persecution.

Jesus said, "Destroy this temple, and I will raise it again in three days" (John 2:19). Jesus ended the era of the *physical* temple. The veil was torn in two. What was previously **separated** became **integrated**. The church was a spiritual family on mission together, a living sacrifice, a humble movement of service and love.

Constantine, however, did not self-identify with Jesus. No, Constantine claimed his Christian roots in Moses, the mighty deliverer, and in David, the great king and conqueror. Like the kings of old, it wasn't right to have a Roman palace without a fitting house for her deity. It was time to rebuild the temple. It was time to rebuild the *fourth place*.

Let's take a look at what happened to the forms of **place, people** and **practices** when the great architect went to work on his Empire-wide temple building project.

Place—Rebuilding the Holy of Holies

Remember the Old Testament temple structures? Remember the concentric circles separating the holy things from the unholy? Constantine rebuilt those.

Where Christians used to meet in *community centers* and homes, Constantine standardized Christian architecture in large, aisled, meeting halls called *basilicas*. The word *basilica* means "royal building."[30] Since the basic form had been in place for centuries, often used for pagan worship, the very architecture represented a blending of Christ, Roman royalty and paganism.

Basilicas themselves were not the whole problem. At least, not in Rome. In Rome, some basilicas were simple covered structures used for many purposes, including business. Christians could have gathered both in simple basilicas and also in homes and stayed relatively integrated with their culture.

The problem with the basilicas was threefold. One, when the basilica was used outside of Rome it no longer integrated with culture but imposed Roman culture. Two, when the basilica was improved upon and made more impressive it no longer reflected integration but Christian imperialism. And three, when the basilica gathering replaced the meal as the central Christian gathering it fundamentally changed the nature of Christianity.

Where before Christians met around tables and a meal, now they would sit in rows, facing a platform. Sound familiar? Not only that, but Constantine insisted that the new basilicas be elevated above the surrounding buildings. What is the message of that medium? The church is now the overseer of culture rather than its servant. If your church steeple or cross or billboard stands over and above your neighbors, you can thank Constantine for that.

Constantine repurposed the basilica as a religious building to separate outsiders from insiders, the clean from the unclean. Heinrich Lützeler describes the impact of the basilica architecture this way: "It exists

---

[30] Jungmann, *The Early Liturgy*, 123.

without the world; it exists against the world, drawing men forcibly inside."[31] The most unclean stayed outside the basilica in the outer courts—yes, they actually built "outer courts" for non-believers, just like the Jerusalem temple. They built separate sections for the *catechumens* (those not yet baptized), for the main congregation of "the faithful," and finally for the most holy group, the clergy. Where leaders in the early church needed no special seats, Constantine's clergy were separated at the front of the hall on a platform. Sound familiar? He even had screens built to visibly separate the clergy from the laity, making the clergy appear even more holy and mysterious.

What impact did the basilica have on Christianity? It was a complete paradigm shift. The primary identity of the church shifted from being **a spiritual family on mission together** to being **an event in a building**.

Acts 20:7 says, "On the first day of the week we came together to break bread." Breaking bread is how Luke described the weekly gathering. "Every day they continued to meet together in the temple courts. They broke bread in their homes and ate together with glad and sincere hearts" (Acts 2:46).

Prior to Constantine, the community was the main thing, and the location was secondary. The church was a WHO, not a WHAT. The location was functional only. The question was, "What type of place will best facilitate the community and our priorities like fellowship, eating and mercy?"

The message of the pagan temples was just the opposite. Temples were about WHAT, not WHO. The glory of the deity was reflected by the building itself and the quality of the ceremony. If the craftsmanship, the cost, the ornamentation, the incense and the music were excellent,

---

[31] Heinrich Lützeler, "Geschichte der christlichen Kunst des Abendlandes" (Bonn, 1932) in Joseph A. Jungmann, *The Early Liturgy*, 124.

then a great God must dwell there. If you wonder why we dress up for church or invest countless dollars in sound systems, it's because we think those things reflect our devotion to God.

Do you see the foundational shift in thinking and practice here? It sounds so noble. Don't we want to display God's glory, after all? Don't we want to build God a lavish home? Doesn't he deserve our excellence? The problem with this line of reasoning is that it is the exact opposite of what the New Testament teaches. God chooses where to display his glory, not us.

Paul writes in 2 Corinthians 4:6-7, "For God, who said, 'Let light shine out of darkness,' made his light shine in our hearts to give us the light of the knowledge of the glory of God in the face of Christ. But we have this treasure in jars of clay to show that this all-surpassing power is from God and not from us."

God chose to display his glory in jars of clay—weak, normal people with nothing impressive on the outside, but who are full of God's Spirit on the inside. God chose the human heart as the dwelling place of his glory, a temple made of flesh.

The true God accepts us as we are—no makeup, no fancy clothes, blemishes and all. God accepts "normal." Not Rome. Rome needed power. Constantine transferred the glory of God from the weak back to the strong; from flesh back to brick and mortar. In doing so, Constantine changed the very foundation of the church.

Constantine's foundational paradigm was this: **Church is primarily an event in a building.** Church would no longer be identified by the people, but by the address. The dwelling place of God moved back into the *fourth place.* Like this:

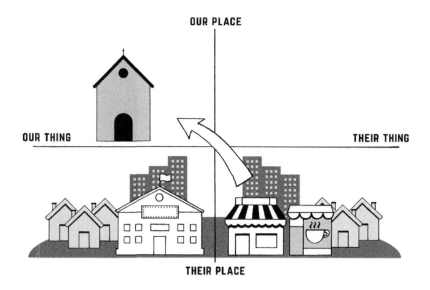

Does someone on your church platform ever say, "Welcome to the house of God"? You can thank Constantine for that. Do you call your meeting place a *sanctuary*, a word meaning *holy place*? Or do you call it a *worship center*? Do we realize that we are telling people that the center of worship is in a building? Do we realize how this violates the most basic New Testament theology of the dwelling place of God?

"Church would no longer be identified by the people but by the address."

Constantine rebuilt the temple.

No longer would "worship in Spirit and truth" be about a mobile temple taking God's glory into the world. In order to worship God, we would again need to come to the particular place, the holy place—the church building.

People—Reinstating the Priesthood

Remember the temple priests? Remember the select class that had access to God while others had to wait outside? Constantine rehired them.

Not only did Constantine rebuild the "house of God," the center of worship, he also rebuilt the altar. Guess where he placed it? Right behind the screen where only the priests had access. Do you see what he did? He separated out a new class of holy people as mediator. He built forms that told common people they could no longer have direct access to God. They couldn't get to the altar on their own. They needed a priest.

In the New Testament, people are the sacrifice and the world is the altar. Believers, rich or poor, righteous or sinful, black or white, male or female, have full-time access to the throne room of God. Hebrews 13:10 says, "We have an altar from which those who minister at the tabernacle have no right to eat."

Constantine disagreed. He rebuilt a physical altar. Does your church have one too? Is it up front near your preacher? What does it look like? Is it steps ascending to your platform? Is it a table? Do you give "altar calls"? Where do people go? Toward the front? Toward the holy man?

Constantine put the Holy of Holies back in business and restitched the curtain Jesus tore apart. Guess what were added as decorative elements onto many of the screens? Cherubim. The same Cherubim that kept Adam and Eve out of Eden and common people out of the Holy of Holies now separated the clergy from the laity.

The work Jesus did on the cross to make a way for everyone right into the very throne room of God was despised in favor of a new hierarchy. The new altar was just as inaccessible to the congregation as was the ark of the covenant to the Jews. In a matter of decades, the New Testament priesthood of all believers, the beautifully diverse temple of the Holy Spirit, was redivided into holy and unholy, clean and unclean, Jew and Gentile, male and female.

Not only were priests given a new level of holiness, they were also given political power. Constantine considered himself the thirteenth apostle, Christ's vicar on earth, the Seat of Justice, the Invincible Sun who was divinely chosen to lead Christ's church to victory over her enemies.[32] With such glorious titles, how could the rest of the clergy class escape his efforts to make the religious elite worthy of the Empire? He elevated his church leaders in the same way he elevated himself, giving them rank and privilege as government officials. The church leadership structure already mirrored that of the Empire, with town and parish clergy, provincial bishops and major "holy sees" in dominant church centers such as Alexandria, Rome and Constantinople. When Rome married Christ, it was only natural to also grant local church leaders political authority to match their regional church influence.

Jesus encouraged his followers not to choose the best seats.[33] Constantine disagreed. Instead, "The bishop, clad in the garments of a high magistrate, entered the church in solemn procession, preceded by the insignia of his official rank, candles and book. Flanked by his presbyters, he was seated on a throne...."[34]

Constantine took all the cultural flavor, humility, beauty and variety out of the early church, systematized it, polished it and professionalized it. In the early church, leaders served from within the community. People

---

[32] Krautheimer, *Early Christian and Byzantine Architecture*, 39.
[33] Luke 14 describes a meal Jesus shared at the home of a prominent Pharisee. "When [Jesus] noticed how the guests picked the places of honor at the table, he told them this parable: 'When someone invites you to a wedding feast, do not take the place of honor...But when you are invited, take the lowest place...For everyone who exalts himself will be humbled" (Luke 14:7-11).
[34] Krautheimer, *Early Christian and Byzantine Architecture*, 40.

with normal jobs, families and character served as elders—no specialized training required. Look at Paul's list to Timothy of the requirements of an elder and you will see that most of the qualifications pertain to integrity, life experience and family (1 Tim. 3:1-7).

When Constantine professionalized the clergy, the amount of training and specialization increased exponentially. Church became a show containing all the flair of the Imperial Court. Just like the Levites of old, only a select class of trained professionals were up to the new performance standards.

How much time, energy, stress and budget does your church dedicate toward making Sunday a good performance? You can thank Constantine for that. Paul's churches were led by faithful men and women with normal lives and good reputations in the neighborhood. Constantine's clergy became a new class of Christian celebrities.

Practices—Reinstating the Sacrifice

Remember the sacrifices and offerings of the Old Testament temple? Constantine reinstated those too. Not content with the humble and highly participatory meals, scripture readings, teaching, prayer and charity of the early Christian gatherings, Constantine needed it bigger and better. More expensive. More elaborate. Christ's glory demands it!

He had already designed architecture to draw people into the most holy place. He had already elevated his priests as celebrity mediators. What more could he do to draw his masses into his new basilica and unite the Empire under one religion? Simple: turn a community meal into a magic show. Give the bread and the wine the mysterious power to take away sins. Still not enough? Give bread the power to heal!

The liturgy of the new *mass* ran through a litany of rituals, climaxing in the *elevation of the host*, the raising of the bread and wine by the priest. Behind their secret screen, the holy people in the most holy place raised the holy elements toward heaven and consecrated them. In this act, the common bread and wine became the very body and blood of Jesus himself, endowed with special powers for the forgiveness and healing of those present. Over time, people came to believe that the ritual itself had the power to forgive sins, free people from physical suffering, even release relatives from purgatory.[35]

The Old Testament sacrificial system had returned, this time not with bulls or goats, but with bread and wine. Now as a mockery of Jesus' final sacrifice, *the mass* became a religious work, a repeated sacrifice necessary to attain grace. The community meal to remember Jesus' completed work on the cross was replaced by a theater of superstition.

"The community meal to remember Jesus' completed work on the cross was replaced by a theater of superstition."

Everywhere Rome spread, the church spread. Everywhere the church spread, the mass was used as the standard liturgy. Regardless of context, regardless of language or custom, the standardized mass in the Roman Latin was performed from Bethlehem to Barcelona.

In the early church, variety was the norm. The church was a community, a spiritual family. Families look different in North Africa than they do in Rome. Practices varied. Liturgy varied. The gathering reflected the diversity of the culture. When Constantine changed the foundation of the church, all of this beautiful variety was swallowed up by uniformity.

---

[35] Robert E. Webber, *Worship Old and New: A Biblical, Historical, and Practical Introduction* (Grand Rapids: Zondervan, 1994), 104.

What Jesus had built as a spiritual family integrated into the fabric of culture, Constantine converted back into **a holy place where holy people do holy things**. Christianity, the humble faith of a suffering servant, came to be seated on a throne of gold, surrounded by a celebrity entourage, and enforced through military power.

A Look in the Mirror

Constantine rebuilt the church as a temple, a mockery of Jesus and gospel. The gospel says:

> *You are reconciled to God.*
> *You have a new community of brothers and sisters.*
> *You have a purpose in the world.*

Constantine's forms said the opposite:

> *You are separated from God.*
> *People are divided into clergy and laity.*
> *The world is divided into sacred and secular.*

The Old Testament temple made sense. The message was consistent. We were separated from God and the forms reinforced the message. Not so with Constantine's temple. The *fourth place* would now be a place of mixed messages; a place of confusion.

Of course, it was not all Constantine's fault. It was happening prior to his reign and it continued after his death. What Constantine spearheaded many others continued as Christendom, the spread of Christianity through the power of the state. The movement continued for another millennium and continues to influence us today.

Constantine and Christendom embody the origins of the modern *fourth place*. Be aware that it likely would have happened with or without Constantine. The history of the faith is a constant cycle of the death of true faith through power and the reawakening of faith through the Spirit of Christ. If we take an honest look in the mirror, we can see the inclination toward separation in all of us. We all deal with the lust for notoriety and personal gain. We all want to distinguish the clean from the unclean, the holy insiders from the unholy outsiders. We are all drawn to the impressive.

Separation is easy. Separation is in our nature from the garden. **Integration** is much harder. The way of Christ is to walk humbly—to serve, to pray, to look to the unseen God in the midst of the weak rather than the strong, to promote others instead of ourselves. Let us take a look at our own heart as we continue the journey.

A Major Fixer-Upper

Now some of you may be wondering about the Reformation. Didn't the Reformation fix most of these issues? That is a very complex question, but the short answer is *not as much as you might think*. While monumental reform took place in theology and content, changes to the medium were more slow and varied.

One way to think about it is this—if Constantine was the temple architect and Christendom was the temple builder, then the Reformers were the temple remodelers. By the 1500s, the church was a major fixer-upper and each of the Reformers had their own ideas of what should stay, what should go, what should be painted over and what should be razed to the ground.

Luther was a "coat of paint" kind of guy. He sandblasted Catholic theology, but in terms of the medium he kept the basic service order, building and decor just about the same.

Calvin was more of a "down to the studs" remodeler. He stripped the organs and icons but mostly just traded the elevation of the host (the climax of the mass) for the elevation of the pulpit. People used to show up late to catch the elevation. Now they would show up late to catch the sermon.[36]

Despite all of the fighting and war and more fighting, most of the remodels were cosmetic in nature. The free church movement probably did the most to address the underlying medium, but most of the changes of the Reformation were just tweaks made to the same basic temple wineskin. Church generally remained **a holy place where holy people do holy things**.

The Reformed church kept the Ave Maria (Latin for "Hail, Mary") as part of the liturgy for forty years. Zwingli corrected the theology of the prayers of the mass but left them in Latin. Calvin, to his chagrin, only took communion four times a year. One Reformer moved the baptismal font next to the pulpit. Another kept the font near the church entrance. One added congregational singing. One said the Lord's Prayer in Latin. Another said it in French. Another removed it altogether.[37]

A lot changed, and a lot didn't. Why were the Reformers able to do so little with the medium? Because when the pendulum swings so far over a thousand years to the side of holy places, holy people and holy practices, it can hardly be expected that one or even ten generations can make such a monumental correction so quickly. Though the Reformers did a great deal in the realm of theology, they left Constantine's basic forms and foundations largely untouched. We will see as we transition to Part 2 of the book that despite the best efforts of the Reformers, the influence of Constantine and Christendom is still alive and well in the modern church.

---

[36] From Robert Kingdom "Worship in Geneva Before and After the Reformation" in Karin Maag and John D. Witvliet, Editors. *Worship in Medieval and Early Modern Europe: Change and Continuity in Religious Practice* (Notre Dame: University of Notre Dame Press, 2004), 52-53.
[37] James F. White, *Protestant Worship* (Louisville, KY: Westminster/John Knox Press, 1989).

PART 2

THE 4TH PLACE TODAY

5

Welcome to the Club

You remember sociologist Ray Oldenburg's model describing the various places that people live, work and play. The *first place* is the home—**private life**. The *second place* is work or school—**productive life**. The *third place* is the pub, the café, the park—what he calls **informal public life**.

Oldenburg's focus in his book, *The Great Good Place*, is on the *third place*. He lets you experience the smells, tastes, laughter and conversation of the French café, the historic German-American beer garden and the English pub. When I first read his book, my longing to hang out in these *third places* was palpable.

But I am not writing about the *third place*. I am writing about the *fourth place*.

I am making the case that there should be a fourth category. If there is a category called *informal public life*, the *third place*, then there should be a counterpart called *formal public life,* the *fourth place*. As we have discovered, the church is part of this fourth category, the *fourth place*.

This is not where we are meant to be. Jesus moved the temple out of the *fourth place*, the physical building, and into a mobile community. Yet, today, the *fourth place* is where we are—right alongside country clubs, stadiums, and other places of insiders and outsiders, people with tickets and those out of luck.

Oldenburg never uses the term, *fourth place*, but at one point he contrasts the English pub, a thriving *third place*, against the English club, a *fourth place* for England's elite:

> The land of the pub is also the land of the club. They are polar opposites. The former helped England into her modern democracy while the latter still epitomizes the divisiveness of England's long-standing and notorious stratification system. The word club derives from the Anglo-Saxon *clifan* or *cleofian* (literally, our cleave)[38]—the word cleave meaning both "to divide" and "to adhere." Thus, *club* represents a unity achieved for the purpose of division. The English club has served both to symbolize and enforce England's long tradition of inequality.[39]

He goes on to say, "The snubs and smugs have exclusive clubs, but the soul of England resides in her pubs."[40] Not only does it rhyme but it's also true! And not just about England. The soul of your city, your town, your community is also in her public life. Regardless, for most of us, that's not where the church lives. No, instead we are Oldenburg's club.

We are the event in the building.

---

[38] John Timbs, *Clubs and Club Life in London* (Detroit; Gale Research Company, 1967), 2-3, in Ray Oldenburg, *The Great Good Place*, 123.
[39] Oldenburg, *The Great Good Place*, 123.
[40] Oldenburg, 123.

This chapter begins Part 2 of our journey through church media. Part 1 told the story of how the church got into the *fourth place*. Part 2 will detail the enormous impact of the *fourth place* on today's church. We will spend one chapter on each medium: **place, people** and **practices**.

We begin here with **place**. The primary impact of Constantine on the church regarding **place** is that he changed the very definition of church from a community to a building—the *fourth place*. Constantine, the architect, built us a beautiful club—complete with an impressive and elaborately decorated clubhouse. The church left the regular rhythms of the *first, second* and *third places* and the world was redivided into sacred and secular. As Oldenburg says, "a unity achieved for the purpose of division." In the process the church received a new mission. Rather than seeing the kingdom of God spread into the diverse beauty of every culture, every place, our unintentional mission would be to get people to join our largely homogenous clubs.

Attractional by Nature

To incarnate is to become human. In the incarnation, Jesus left his heavenly throne and entered the mess of culture. He ate in homes, worked as a carpenter, and hung out on the shore of the Sea of Galilee and in the Garden of Gethsemane. Jesus lived his life among Jewish *first, second* and *third* places. Everything he did was about going to people, not expecting them to come to him. This is what it means to be **incarnational**. We enter the world of the people we want to love and impact. We don't invite people to come to a holy place; the holy place goes to them.

"We don't invite people to come to a holy place; the holy place goes to them."

Attractional is just the opposite. In attractional ministry, the church building is seen as the holy center. Our efforts draw people toward our programs inside our buildings. We use personal invitations, mailers, signage, social media and other means to get them to come to us. The website, the parking lot, the lobby and the seating design all move people from the outside to the inside.

Many churches and leaders are already aware of this. They have already identified their attractional tendencies and may have even adjusted their logo or preached a sermon series using words like *missional* and *incarnational.* What we often fail to realize, however, is that we cannot become incarnational simply by preaching different sermons or adjusting our mission statement. The medium is the message and *fourth places* are attractional by nature.

The Rules of the Fourth Place

Fourth places, by their very existence, pull people toward their center. Why? Because we must convince people to leave their normal lives and join us in OUR PLACE. Like this:

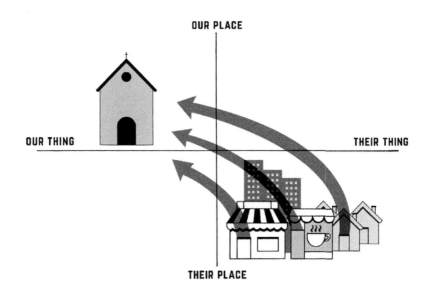

Clubs, teams, events and associations all vie for the time of already busy people. So do churches. We purchase advertising space, billboards and commercials. We pour our hearts into our logos and branding. Why? Because we have a difficult job. We must convince people that our *fourth place* is worth their time. Once we have them inside, the task is equally difficult. We must convince them that we are superior to the competition. We must convince people to stay and pay. Our financial bottom line, our very survival, depends on their paying membership.

We use more spiritual words than these, of course, but anyone in ministry understands the pressure to self-promote. Why do we do this? The reason is simple—the church now occupies the *fourth place* and therefore must operate according to the rules of the *fourth place*. If you work for a church and regret having to spend so much time, money and personnel on branding, marketing, video and production, the inconvenient truth is that as long as we occupy the *fourth place*, these functions will be our priority. It's in the *fourth place* DNA.

A Church Without a Footprint

While we are so used to churches as centers of self-promotion, let's stop and think for a minute.

Can you imagine Jesus handing out flyers for an event?
Can you imagine Jesus hyping up an upcoming concert?
Can you imagine Jesus wearing a church T-shirt with an awesome cross logo?

Of course not—and it's not just because they weren't invented yet. The reason is because Jesus became a part of the world he wanted to touch. He didn't stand out and draw attention to himself through clever marketing. Clearly, mobs of people followed him everywhere. People tend to do that when you are healing their children and filling their starving stomachs. Yet in all of this, Jesus never self-promoted. When they wanted to make him king by force, he walked away. When they wanted him to perform, he refused. Jesus was not trying to get people to come to a separate place or event; he was trying to integrate his life with theirs.

I want to share one of my favorite patristic writings. It is known as "The Letter to Diognetus" and was likely written around 130 AD by someone who identifies himself simply as *a disciple of the apostles*. It explains the early Christian attitude toward integration better than I ever could.

> Christians cannot be distinguished from the rest of humankind by country, speech, or customs. They do not live in cities of their own; they do not speak a special language; they do not follow a peculiar manner of life. Their teaching was not invented by the ingenuity or speculation of men, nor do they advocate mere book learning, as other groups do.
>
> They live in Greek cities and they live in non-Greek cities according to the lot of each one. They conform to the customs of their country in dress, food, and the general mode of life, and yet they show a remarkable, and admittedly extraordinary structure of their own life together. They live in their own countries, but only as guests and aliens. They take part in everything as citizens and endure everything as aliens. Every foreign country is their homeland, and every homeland is a foreign country to them.
>
> They marry like everyone else. They beget children, but they do not expose them after they are born. They have a common table, but no common bed. They live in the flesh, but they do not live according to the flesh. They live on earth, but their citizenship is in heaven. They obey the established laws, but through their way of life they surpass these laws. They love all people and are persecuted by all. Nobody knows them, and

yet they are condemned. They are put to death, and just through this they are brought to life. They are poor as beggars, and yet they make many rich...

...In a word: what the soul is in the body, the Christians are in the world. As the soul is present in all the members of the body, so Christians are present in all the cities of the world. As the soul lives in the body, yet does not have its origin in the body, so the Christians live in the world yet are not of the world. Invisible, the soul is enclosed by the visible body: in the same way the Christians are known to be in the world, but their religion remains invisible.[41]

Did you catch that last line, "...their religion remains invisible"? Can you imagine that? A church without walls, without a big cross out front, without T-shirts and bumper stickers. A church not known by its merchandise and paraphernalia, but by the good it does for the world in which it resides.

When Christianity is called *invisible*, some will be cautious because people have at times used the term, *the invisible church*, to argue that Christians do not need to be a part of a community, a gathered church. "My church is the mountains," they say. Of course Christians need to gather. We are a spiritual family, not isolated individuals.

By calling the church *invisible*, the writer above is not arguing for Christians to avoid gathering. He is simply saying that Christians are not meant to be a separate subculture in their own place, but a redemptive community knit into the prevailing culture.

How did they live like this in the early church?

---

[41] "The Epistle of Mathetes to Diognetus," v and vi, in Eberhard Arnold, *The Early Christians in Their Own Words*, 114-115.

To stretch the imagination, I want to show the same graphic as above, and now reveal where the early church fits on the chart.

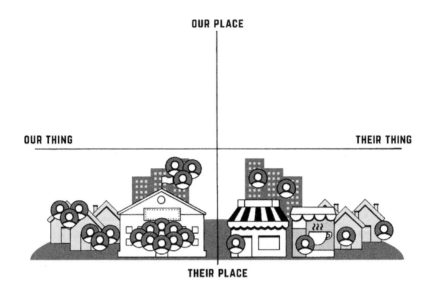

The early church had no *fourth place*, no religious zone. They only occupied the bottom two quadrants.

They incarnated themselves into their world like Jesus. They still gathered, but they gathered in nonreligious spaces—the OUR THING, THEIR PLACE quadrant. This does not mean they never gathered in buildings. It means they did not create religious buildings called churches. Church was a WHO, not a WHAT.

I show groups on the left side and scattered dots on the right side to show that the church was the church whether they were gathered or scattered. Church was not primarily an event but a spiritual family. Families are still families whether they are doing things like communion, prayer and teaching in buildings, or simply living their normal lives together.

The early church had no OUR PLACE quadrants. The top half of this chart didn't even exist. Can you imagine your Christian experience without your building?

Now, I want to be clear. God has done wonderful things in our buildings. I have been very impacted personally in religious buildings. I was raised there, went to youth group there, and have had significant encounters with God there. For centuries, people have been experiencing God within the walls of church structures. God has used those buildings to serve our people, our communities and our world in profound ways. This book is about a change in wineskin, not a change in wine. God has used our media to produce some beautiful wine.

Regardless, I want to talk about the message of our medium, or wineskin. What are our buildings saying? What is the world hearing? These questions become more important the wider the cultural gap grows between those inside the building and those outside it.

To the degree that our buildings communicate that they are holy places, they inadvertently (and sometimes advertently!) communicate that every other place is unholy. That's what temple media do. By creating a holy inside, they naturally create an unholy outside. The nature of the club is to divide—insiders from outsiders, sacred from secular.

Jesus came to proclaim a different message: *I love you before you get cleaned up. I don't need you to leave your world; I will teach you to redeem your world from the inside out.*

Think of how the message of a church gathering in a school differs from a religious building. Listen to the message inherent in the school medium: *God cares about the world of our kids. God cares about education—not just Bible studies, but math, and history and languages. The God that created science is actually pleased when his children study it.*

What about the message of a church gathered in a theater? *God loves the arts. Not just the ones labeled "Christian" but ones that value the whole human experience of love, anger, beauty, tragedy and death. God so values the human experience that he became a tragedy for us. He became death for us. Jesus, the Word of God, the radiance of his glory, a walking masterpiece.*

Do you see it? Christ himself came to affirm and redeem the human condition, not separate us from it. When we live and gather within cultural spaces we proclaim the message of Jesus: God loved us enough to leave his own place and come to where we are. He became Emmanuel, God with us.

The great irony is that when the church becomes invisible, entwined with the places of culture, Jesus finally becomes visible. People can finally see a God who cares about his beloved creation enough to get his hands dirty in it.

"When the church becomes invisible...Jesus finally becomes visible."

Church in Other Places
by Dudley Callison

The church becomes a powerful revelation of Christ when it happens within the normal rhythms of life. Rather than "going to church," we become spiritual family right where people live. In the *first place*, the phenomenon of house church or what we call Neighbor Church in my neighborhood is simply the gathering of people who share their faith with others who live nearby. Even if some attend church elsewhere on Sunday or don't attend at all, the opportunity to share spiritual life with those we live near becomes a springboard to deeper community, healthier neighborhoods, and serving those nearby in need. In the second place, work, businesses can offer employees the opportunity to participate in pre-work Bible studies, informal social gatherings and community service projects. We recently established a coworking space where people can pursue their occupational dreams in a supportive community. Some coworkers know Christ and see this as a primary place to introduce others to a faith-oriented life.

We also see this happening in the third place—faith community built around common interests. "Churches" are popping up among motorcycle clubs, fitness centers, local pubs, RV and camping groups, even NASCAR fans! Wherever believers gather with shared interests, they can also share their interest in Christ, inviting others to participate who are still on the journey of faith.

The best place for the church is as a redemptive community embedded within, not separated from, culture. We hear this concept echoed in the teachings of Jesus. Jesus said that the kingdom is like yeast in dough. You cannot see the yeast, but it causes the bread to rise. It fills the whole room with a delicious fragrance, even though it's invisible. Jesus said the kingdom is like salt. It makes everything taste delicious, but all you see is the food, not the salt itself.

Christendom separated Christians into their own club. To stay with Jesus' metaphor, this would be like separating salt from food. Salt is wonderful as long as it is flavoring and preserving food; salt by itself is disgusting. Yeast is miraculous when it makes bread rise; yeast by itself is useless.

Unfortunately, to many in our culture, Christians and their buildings are just as useless. An unsightly blight on the city. A parking annoyance. An unfortunate city planning or zoning decision. Rather than observing a humble community loving and serving our neighborhoods, they see us striving for bigger and better buildings and performances. Wouldn't we rather they see Jesus? I wonder if our attractional nature might be backfiring on us.

The Fourth Place Unleashed

Attractional meant one thing in Constantine's day. People didn't have cars. They simply stuck a towering building in the city center, rang a bell, and the people came. The church was all Roman Catholic so there was really no competition to worry about.

Today, however, we are dealing with **attractional** on steroids. Why? For one, we have a growing cultural gap between the *fourth place* and its surrounding culture. The greater the cultural distance between church insiders and "secular" outsiders, the harder we have to work to attract them. Add to that the reality that we are consumer-driven and celebrity-obsessed. Add to that the fact that we are competing with one another for limited human market share, and it is no wonder we now have *fourth places* outshining the Tower of Babel!

A senior pastor of a church in Texas once described his church as "a town within a city." They have a $50+ million dollar annual budget and more than 20,000 attendees. Their campus includes a massive worship complex, a fitness center, a bookstore and a café. When asked to explain why they need all of the excess, the pastor responded, "God's house ought to be beautiful."[42]

---

[42]Jesse Bogan, "America's Biggest Megachurches," *Forbes* June 26, 2009, http://www.forbes.com/2009/06/26/americas-biggest-megachurches-business-megachurches.html.

Constantine would be so proud.

Not coincidentally, the same trend toward bigger and better exists in other *fourth place* industries. Hotels are competing for the most amenities while multibillion dollar stadiums race for the most exotic fan features. In the country club industry, medium-sized clubs are closing while all-inclusive megaclubs are ever expanding. Sound familiar? In all *fourth places*, attraction is the name of the game.

In an attempt to maintain this level of attractiveness, church budgets and staff are forced to spend their resources keeping up their *fourth place* image rather than focusing on social justice, discipleship and mission.

Small churches are not immune either. Most small churches actually spend a higher percentage on staff and buildings than megachurches. A pastor of a small church recently told me that most of their congregation moved out of their part of town more than twenty years ago seeking nicer neighborhoods. These commuters still attend their church building Sunday mornings, Sunday nights and Wednesday nights. Many of their leaders add an additional one to three nights on top of that! Ironically, none of them live anywhere near the church building, some driving up to an hour. This small "church" is churning through enormous resources of time and money and is making virtually zero positive impact on their neighborhood.

The majority of churches in the United States have between fifty and one hundred people and most of those people are between the ages of fifty and one hundred. It's not that small churches are avoiding being attractional, it's that they are losing the attraction battle. While there are many great exceptions of small churches deeply integrated into their communities, especially in rural areas, many small churches are simply no longer attractive and are having to close their doors. *Fourth place* churches are exhausting themselves building better temples (or clinging to small old ones) while Jesus told us that we are to *be* the temple.

From Attractional to Extractional

Hopefully, you are starting to see the direct link from church in the *fourth place* to our **attractional** missiology—the way we do our mission. Unfortunately, Constantine's impact does not stop there. Our entire way of being the church, our ecclesiology, also comes from our nature as a *fourth place*. Alan Hirsch refers to our ecclesiology as **extractional**.[43]

Think, for example, of how we typically practice *discipleship*. We remove, or **extract**, people from their *first*, *second* and *third places* and ask them to come to a *fourth place* to grow more like Jesus. Certainly, churches with strong small group ministries or missional communities meeting in homes are moving in the right direction. They are getting people into the *first place* together. Still, most churches use their buildings for almost everything—classes, services, Bible studies, men's and women's ministry events, you name it.

Our primary mode of discipleship is extractional. We leave our families, wave to our neighbors, drive past the homeless, the workplace, the coffee shop, and the park, on our way to the *fourth place*.

Our missiology is **attractional**. Our ecclesiology is **extractional**.

Our entire system is built to separate us from culture. We worship in the *fourth place*. We serve in the *fourth place*. We give to the *fourth place*. Church success has largely been determined by attendance and giving to the *fourth place*. Discipleship has been measured by Bible study hours logged in the *fourth place*. Evangelism means inviting people into the *fourth place*. It's no surprise we end up with more consumers than disciples.

---

[43] Alan Hirsch, *The Forgotten Ways: Reactivating the Missional Church* (Grand Rapids, MI: Brazos Press, 2006).

To make disciples, Jesus called people out of the crowds and onto the road. They watched him, walked with him and healed with him. In the process, he wore down their racist, materialistic, religious selves until they had nothing left but love.

Discipleship for Jesus was all about being a spiritual family right in the midst of culture. It was about a community of people taking risks in the real world with real people and real problems. It had very little to do with sitting in chairs in rows in a building. Service for Jesus was about justice for the oppressed, not becoming efficient parking lot attendants or tackling sound issues.

We have built *fourth place* programs and called them *evangelism* and *discipleship*. One tries to save people and the other tries to grow people. Evangelism and discipleship, at their best, are not programs; they are part of a way of life in community. The reason the word *evangelism* gives people PTSD is because we made it into a program and we made people our projects.

It was never meant to be this way.

Jesus lived among people and loved them. They were attracted to his extraordinary way of life like thirsty people to a glass of cold water. It was natural, not forced. It was real, not artificial.

The Nature of Christianity

Christianity in its nature is not an event in a building, but a people movement. It is not a subculture of people who like all of the same types of nonoffensive music or nonvulgar language or nondancing bodies. We are not cultural separationists. We are salt, and light and yeast. We do not extract; we incarnate.

We are not building owners; we are neighborhood stewards.

We are the faith that didn't even have a name for its first decades. The early believers identified themselves as part of *the way*.

It was years until they would first be called *Christians*. Even then, the name simply referred to their identity as followers of Christ, not a separate religion.

Other religions look to their center when they pray; we look to our Father who is unseen. Other religions follow a guru in a holy building; we follow the way of life of a homeless man. Every other religion connects the place of its founder's life events, and particularly their death, with its religious center. Christians don't have a Mecca. Christians don't even know where Jesus died and was buried! (The tour guide will tell you they do, but they don't.) Christians didn't even honor holy places until Constantine. In fact, it was his mother, Helena, who enshrined what she thought were the holiest places of Christianity— The Church of the Holy Sepulchre (the tomb), The Church of the Nativity, and more.

Constantine commissioned basilicas to be built right on top of these holy sites. Talk about a cultural footprint! He built Rome right on top of Bethlehem. That is not irony, friends. That is a sign of the new wineskin under Constantine called Christendom, where Christianity imposes culture rather than integrates with culture.

Jesus described his kingdom as yeast working through the entire batch of dough. He did not describe his kingdom as a gigantic loaf of bread bejeweled with fruit and nuts, squashing all of the smaller loaves into submission.

The "Letter to Diognetus" above should not be shocking if we are students of the New Testament. Hebrews 11:13-16 describes the people of faith:

All these people were still living by faith when they died. They did not receive the things promised; they only saw them and welcomed them from a distance. And they admitted that they were aliens and strangers on earth. People who say such things show that they are looking for a country of their own. If they had been thinking of the country they had left, they would have had opportunity to return. Instead, they were longing for a better country—a heavenly one. Therefore God is not ashamed to be called their God, for he has prepared a city for them.

Christians are not destined to have their perfect dream home now. We are not supposed to sit back in our comfortable megachurch complexes.

We are strangers on earth. We are a unique community but without our own unique place. We sacrifice for each other more than those in a club ever would, but we refuse to build ourselves a clubhouse. We don't need the *fourth place*. We can walk together as a community within the streets, homes, alleys, hospitals and warehouses of our existing culture.

As a church, we have drafted our own architecture, developed our own language and created our own music subculture. We have separate schools, separate bookstores, separate clothing lines, separate movies, separate artwork, everything! You name it, we have a Christian version of it.

Of course, the choices we have made to separate from culture are not all black and white. These are hard decisions. We may be making them because we think they will make us or our children more holy or more safe. Regardless, Jesus is praying something different for us. In John 17:15-18, Jesus prays, "My prayer is not that you take them out of the world but that you protect them from the evil one. They are not of the world, even as I am not of it. Sanctify them by the truth; your word is truth. As you sent me into the world, I have sent them into the world."

Christians must live with an unresolvable tension. We are not comfortable in the world. We want our own place, but we can't have our own place. At least not yet.

Didn't Jesus long for his own home? "Foxes have holes and birds of the air have nests, but the Son of Man has no place to lay his head" (Luke 9:58). Didn't Paul want a comfortable home while he languished in prison? Of course, but in the meantime he was loving and serving his guards, reaching the members of Caesar's household with the gospel, and writing letters that make up half of the New Testament!

A Visible Community

When my family moved into our Tacoma, Washington, neighborhood with six other families, we did so intentionally to place our community in the midst of people who did not know Christ. We didn't have a building to worry about. We were free to invest in our neighborhood. We served neighbors, threw block parties and joined the existing rhythms of the community. Eventually, one of our group members headed up Safe Streets, a program to help neighbors watch out for each other. Another teamed up with neighbors to spearhead the annual garage sale. Still another started a club at the local elementary school where many kids got to meet Jesus.

When Christianity became invisible by being worked into the "dough" of our neighborhood, people around us could finally see Christ. Neighbors watched as we walked to each other's homes for our weekly meal. They saw us clean up a neighbor's back yard full of old mattresses and a decade's worth of an abusive husband's junk. As our neighbors saw us, their casual observations turned to curiosity, curiosity to relationship, and relationship to discipleship. We didn't have a building we needed to attract them to, and we didn't have to extract them out of their world. Jesus came to them. How? Through us.

That is how a Christian approach to **place** is supposed to work.

This is true not just of house churches. Do you need a larger place for your gatherings? Rather than creating another church building on another corner, consider asking the question, "What does my neighborhood need?" Does your community need a place for kids after school? Maybe you build a community center—a *third place* instead of a *fourth place*. Does your neighborhood have people commuting hours away from their families for work? Maybe you build a coworking space—a *second place*—and gather there with your community during non-work hours. Or a medical clinic. Or a coffee shop.

Better still, are you sure you need to own the building? Why not join people where they already are? Consider renting a place that already exists. Maybe there is a school available that would appreciate the extra rental income. Maybe there is a back room of a coffee shop. If you need a larger space, consider a convention center or hotel conference space.

Whatever you build or rent, don't build it above them, build it *among* them, *with* them and *for* them. Let your medium speak a new message: God still loves his good creation enough to become a part of it.

Where Are We Going?

For some of you, this is a very new way of thinking about church. For others, you have been in this dialogue for a long time. You are excited that we have named some of the issues you have felt. Perhaps you have been frustrated by church and now you are starting to dream again.

Others will feel a little (or maybe a lot) of frustration. Maybe you agree with some or all of the problems I have presented. Okay, we are attractional. We are extractional.

What in the world am I supposed to do about it?

I will make no apologies that this book is all about change. I am pushing pretty hard at times on some long-accepted ways of being. Although I am an idealist, I also understand a little bit about reality in the church. While God might be inspiring some of you toward radical, wineskin-altering changes, he might be stirring others toward more incremental or slower changes. This book will be helpful for both.

We will go deep into the question, "How do we structure a church for the modern world that occupies only the bottom two quadrants?" It would look like this:

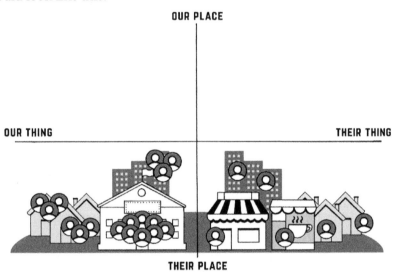

However, we will also ask the question, "What can established building-based churches do to make their forms, their media, speak a better message of integration?" It's not like God hasn't used our buildings in amazing ways in the past. Of course he has! But what can we do to help reach this next generation and align our media with our message?

Hint: it will have largely to do with shifting our emphasis in one, two or all three of these directions:

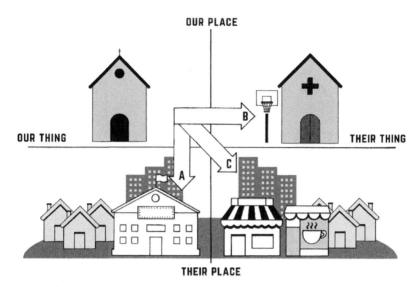

Where Are You?

Ok, so that's where we're headed. Where are you now? In order to get anywhere, we first need to know where we are starting out. You have a unique situation. Your starting point is different from anyone else's reading this book. In order to seek God's direction for change, you first need to orient yourself as to your current church reality.

Below, I will present a few common models of church and where they live on our chart. As we go through these options, I hope you will ask yourself where your past or current experience of church fits. You could even go ahead and put an "X" on the chart to mark your starting place.

OUR THING, OUR PLACE

The first option is the one we've been talking about the most. Maybe when I described the *fourth place* church, it was a no-brainer. You thought, "Yes, that's us. It feels like everything about our church focuses on the event in the building. Our budget, time and stress all point toward the weekend service."

If that's true, you are somewhere in this area.

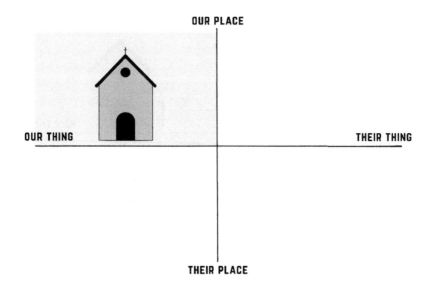

OUR THING, THEIR PLACE

Maybe your church is utilizing the *first place*, the home, for your small groups. Or maybe you meet in a school or other cultural venue for your gathering. If so, you might be somewhere in this gray region:

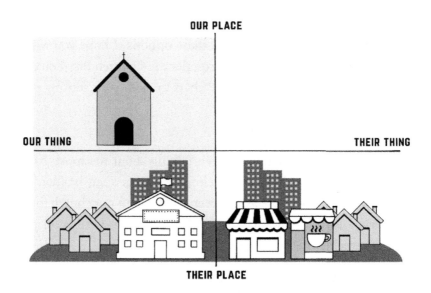

There is a broad range to this area. If your church invests a small amount of time in small groups while most of the church energy and senior leadership focus goes toward the building and building-based events, you would still probably locate your church toward the upper range of the gray area.

If, however, your church has a more balanced approach—a "church of groups", a *Simple Church*[44] model, or practices missional communities and huddles (*3DM*[45])—you might identify yourself closer to the bottom of the range.

If you meet in a school and are intentional about integrating with the life and events of that school, that would move you to the right, THEIR THING. If you meet in a school, but that's the extent of the relationship, you would be further left toward OUR THING.

THEIR THING, OUR PLACE

This means that you own the facility, and you allow other nonreligious organizations to do THEIR THING in your building.

Maybe you have a building, but you use it more like a community center. You run a public coffee shop, enjoy positive tenant relationships or house the homeless. Maybe you actually run a functional hospital building or clinic and happen to also use some of the space for church services.

To the degree that your place is a legitimate *first*, *second* or *third* place for someone else, you have moved to the right in this shaded area:

---

[44] Thom S. Rainer and Eric Geiger, *Simple Church* (Nashville, TN: B&H Publishing Group, 2011).

[45] Mike Breen and Steve Cockram, *Building a Discipling Culture* (Pawleys Island, SC: Mike Breen, 2011).

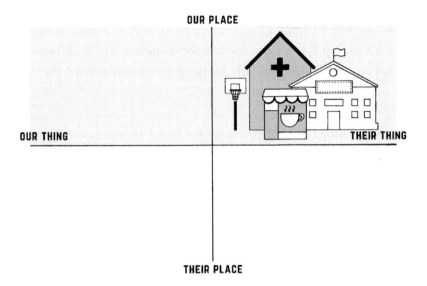

THEIR THING, THEIR PLACE

This is normal life. This is where all humans of all races and religions live, die and pay taxes. Some organizations very intentionally staff their ministries in order to better hang out and love people here. Many parachurch ministries fit this category. Young Life, for example, spends a lot of time and energy on relationships with kids in their world. They go to football games and hang out in school cafeterias. Even senior leaders office at coffee shops. They intentionally structure their organization to **integrate** with the world of the people they are trying to reach. If that's you, maybe you are in this area:

Again, there is a large variance. If your Young Life club meets in a church building, that would push you toward *OUR PLACE*. If your staff is great at contact work—meeting kids on their turf—that would push you toward THEIR PLACE. If you are finding it interesting that the parachurch largely occupies the same space as the early church, keep that thought in mind. There are many lessons the local church can learn from the parachurch as to how to structure themselves to integrate with our world. We will return to this idea later in the book. Along with many parachurch organizations, some missional churches, new monastic communities, and new parish congregations would also locate themselves in this area.

Where are you? Go ahead and mark an "X" on the graphic above to indicate your starting point. You may adjust this as we go along, especially when we factor in the other two media of **people** and **practices**, but this gives you a good way to initially orient yourself for the road ahead.

Fourth Place People

Constantine had a dramatic impact on the modern church. We have now witnessed that impact as it relates to the medium of **place**. Instead of the church living among culture, we have been trying to welcome people to our clubhouse. We have too often become better at salesmanship than discipleship.

Christendom, however, impacted much more than just **place**. Constantine's foundational shift also had a dramatic impact on our very idea of Christian leadership, our **people**. A church operating in the *fourth place* needs a certain type of leader to run it. *Fourth places* are complicated. *Fourth places* are demanding. *Fourth places* need to impress people if they are going to survive. Hiring someone like Jesus simply won't do. You need a Christian celebrity.

6

Hiring: Celebrity Pastor

Our culture is fascinated with celebrities. We take selfies when we come into their proximity. We talk about their outfits and wardrobe failings across cubicle walls. We read about their weddings, divorces, babies and scandals at the checkout aisle. We buy their tickets, scream at the top of our lungs, and wait in line to acquire the t-shirt that proves we were there. We even watch shows where they give awards to themselves.

Why do we do it? Some would argue that we follow big people because we feel small. We participate in another's persona because of a conscious or even subconscious lack in our own lives. In Richard Schickel's fascinating book, *Intimate Strangers*, he tracks the rise of celebrity culture in America over the past one hundred years. He describes one opinion of celebrity as "the power to personify the yearning fantasies of the masses, its ability briefly to fulfill, in largely megafictional terms, their frustrated dreams."[46]

---

[46] Richard Schickel, *Intimate Strangers: The Culture of Celebrity in America* (Ivan R. Dee; Chicago, 2000), 311.

Now, I don't know if a little admiration is such a big deal or if every time we're impressed with someone it reveals a deep psychological need, but I do know that we have a tendency to feel small when we make someone else big. We compare our bodies to our favorite actors and we start to feel ugly. We look at Mark Zuckerberg or Steve Jobs and realize the technology skills or business acumen that we will never possess. We compare our homes to Martha Stewart's or Joanna Gaines's and end up depressed or feeling a strange desire to move to Waco, Texas.

Something about being around greatness makes us feel small, yet we keep coming back for more.

What does this have to do with church? More than you might guess.

In the last chapter about **place,** we discovered that many of our church buildings were not designed to **integrate** with our culture. They were designed to **separate** people from it and bring them into our *fourth places.* In this chapter, we move on to the medium of **people.**

The building was only the beginning of Constantine's impact. In order to run the *fourth place,* Constantine needed a certain type of leader to attract people toward his center. As we will see, Constantine's priests laid the foundation for our modern concept of the role of pastor. This faulty job description has led to our current crisis of discipleship.

A Holy Persona

Why would Constantine want a celebrity at the helm? Because celebrities are uniquely able to draw attention to themselves. Not only that, while celebrities are making themselves larger than life, they also create a sense of deficiency or lack in everyone else. Constantine tapped into this same principle. He was able to control millions of people and keep them continually attached to his centers of worship by creating in them a sense of lack in an area every Christian desires—holiness.

In the Old Testament, the priest was an intermediary, or go-between. The people lacked holiness and needed the priest to fill the gap. So every year they made the trek back to the temple—back to the priest to sacrifice for their sins.

Christ-followers, of course, know that Jesus already dealt with our sin problem once and for all. Jesus is our true priest. Jesus, in fact, is the only true celebrity—the only one whose holiness actually does make up for our lack of holiness. Jesus is the only mediator, the only go-between we will ever need (Heb. 7:24-25).

Constantine was not overly interested in Jesus. Remember, Constantine self-identified with Moses, not Jesus. Who needs a suffering carpenter when you can have the mysterious guy who went up the mountain and came down glowing! After all, a bleeding servant can hardly inspire and unite an empire. Let's be honest, you can't crucify conquered peoples on Roman crosses and then point to your King on that same cross.

Constantine kept people coming back to the mass again and again by making his leaders appear so holy that they were out of reach to the common people. He was not interested in humble servant-leaders; he wanted his religious representatives to look grand and mysterious. He had them march down the center aisle in flowing robes to create a spectacle. Where Jesus said, "Let the little children come unto me," Constantine wanted the kids in the aisle to whisper, "Look, Mom, I almost touched his robe."

Constantine had no desire to grow mature disciples. Community, prayer and sacrificial service toward neighbors held nothing for him. He wanted a simple, dependent people who would keep showing up. Like Marx suggested, he wanted religion as an opiate for the masses. Why is this so important? Because our modern pastoral job description is built on the foundation laid by Constantine's priests. That role was designed not around shepherding souls, but around creating a **holy celebrity persona.**

Designed for Celebrity

Before we go too far, allow me to clarify. I am not saying that every pastor has a hidden agenda to sign autographs or become the next Andy Stanley or Billy Graham. In fact, I would venture to guess that most "celebrity" pastors never intended to become famous. There are many wonderful and humble people leading churches. God has used our pastoral leaders in amazing ways throughout church history and will continue to do so. Remember, the wineskin is not nearly as important as the wine.

However, we have a major systems-level issue that we need to talk about. Our current leadership structures are making it too easy for our leaders to burn out or implode. Why is this happening? Because there are natural power dynamics at work. Remember, the survival of the *fourth place* depends on drawing and keeping people. We need to get them from their world to our world and so we must impress them.

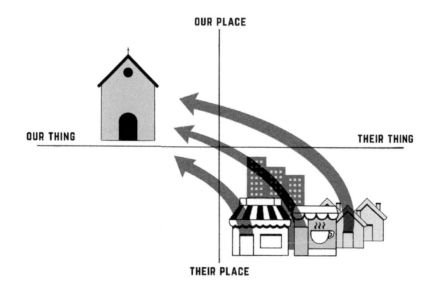

The Bible describes Jesus' life as characterized by downward mobility and kingdom values which are upside down compared to the world's systems of power. Jesus was not physically impressive, nor were most of the people he hung around. While we may preach about this reality, putting it into practice is another venture altogether. After all, we have a *fourth place* image to maintain. In order to draw a crowd, we need our leaders to be the strong face of the organization.

The church human resources guide will tell you the pastor who can draw the bigger crowd should get a bigger paycheck. We flip Jesus' value system back right-side-up, not just because we want to but because we have to if we want to keep attracting the people into our building.

If you are a pastor, you understand this pressure. You feel it when you preach. You feel it from your board or your elders. They want you to be a big deal. If you are an aging pastor, you also feel this stress. Growing churches are hiring young, attractive talent, not well-aged wisdom.

Our church media are still designed for Moses, not Jesus.

Everything from the parking lot, to the aisles, to the service order, all point toward the climax of the service when the holy persona comes down from the mountain, or onto the stage, and delivers the word of the Lord to the crowd of onlookers.

So that the people in the back can see, we project our preachers onto giant screens. While we may think we have done a great credit to the gospel by removing Constantine's curtain separating clergy from laity, is it possible that we have simply traded one screen for another? Is it possible our video screens are performing the same function? Old or new, both screens attest to the reality that the *fourth place* requires us to project a holy persona at our center.

Describing the British Commons Chamber building, Winston Churchill said, "We shape our buildings, and afterward, our buildings shape us." The building with its two inward facing sides ended up shaping the British two-party system.

In the same way, our buildings are driving the type of leader who will be successful in our churches. I was on staff during a megachurch senior pastor transition where the search team kept saying, "We are looking for David, not Saul." They sincerely meant it. However, when you have a giant auditorium, your building has already shaped the person required. Preaching ability was our first filter and everyone who missed the cut was removed from the process. David missed Samuel's first cut too. While Samuel was fawning over Jesse's more impressive son, Eliab (1 Sam. 16:6), David was off in the hills literally pastoring sheep.

We have shaped the *fourth place* and now the *fourth place* is shaping our leaders. And unfortunately, the type of leaders we are shaping are the exact opposite of what we need in order to make disciples. Instead of being led by experienced people capable of guiding us through the challenges of real life in culture, we are being led by a class of religious professionals removed from culture.

Designed to Separate

I remember as a kid, every once in awhile I would bump into a pastor in a public place like a grocery store. My emotional response would tell me, "Pastors are supposed to be in church buildings, not grocery stores." Teachers are supposed to be in schools, doctors in hospitals and pastors in church buildings.

Where does this impression come from? Certainly not from Jesus.

Jesus spent his life in and amongst his culture. He walked their roads, taught in their homes, ate at their tables and prayed in their gardens.

Central to the very identity of Christ himself was the notion that distinctions between the religious elite and the common people were about to be erased. Jesus' disciples, his leaders in training, were a community of nobodies. That was the point.

In the early church every voice mattered and every gift was significant. The church was characterized as a community of mutual participation. There were different roles, but no celebrities. Different gifts, but no platform to ascend. That is what **integration** looks like.

When church became a Roman event, it became so complex that running it required a separate clergy class schooled in the protocol of Rome. The line was redrawn between clergy and laity. Today the line remains because the complexity remains. *Fourth places* are demanding. We require facility upkeep. We have utility bills to pay. We have grounds to maintain. We need sound systems, musicians, ushers and greeters. And don't get me going on children's ministry needs. We always need more nursery workers!

And while you would think that all of this *fourth place* effort should lead to masses of people living like Christ in the world, the opposite is often the case. We are facing a crisis of discipleship in the West.

Discipleship in Crisis

Discipleship is all about modeling. It is the same as parenting. Children follow what parents *do* more than what parents *say*. Modeling overpowers instruction every time. The fundamental flaw of basing church leadership in the *fourth place* is that it is modeling the wrong thing.

We are modeling how to run Christian events rather than how to live like Jesus. The following chart gives some examples. We are modeling public speaking and musicianship for a crowd that needs a whole different set of life skills.

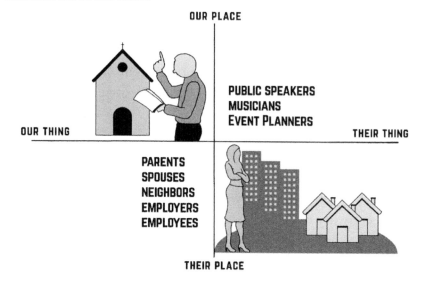

Our pastors are largely modeling how to remove oneself from culture, not how to live within it. Most pastors are supposed to maintain office hours in the *fourth place* and often feel guilty if they leave the building during "work." Their day of rest happens while the world is working, and their work happens while the world is resting. They have separate tax laws. Many of them wear separate clothing, robes or collars.

When the crowd came to arrest Jesus, they weren't sure which one he was. When the crowd comes into our churches, it's pretty obvious who the leader is. He's the guy behind the microphone on the stage with all the lights focused on him.

This disconnect between the *fourth place* and real life is the reason so many kids grow up in our youth groups thinking that to be a strong Christian leader they have to either be a great speaker or a talented musician. The medium is the message, and from youth through adulthood, our media are saying, "If you are serious about your faith, you will leave the world and get trained for the church stage."

While I was working in the corporate world, I had some amazing experiences where God showed up in my workplace. When a non-believer in the cubicle next to me discovered that she had a tumor in her neck and was weeping uncontrollably, a bunch of us Christians invited her to pray with us in one of our conference rooms. She came back a week later and reported that the tumor was gone and she wanted to talk about Jesus.

I also got to sit on a philanthropy committee that decided where to give away hundreds of thousands of dollars a year toward local community needs. I got to help lead two coworker friends to Christ as we ate lunch together every day of the week. In the midst all of that, the work itself was also quite interesting. I got to help build custom IT solutions that made our trading floor more productive.

That whole time I longed for a mentor. I wanted someone to care about the impact I could make as a kingdom-minded businessman. Unfortunately, my pastors weren't really equipped for this. Our church simply wasn't structured to be able to take that type of interest in people. Most churches are in a similar situation. Church leaders treat the work in the *fourth place* as if it's the real work of the ministry. Many pastors are so busy maintaining the fourth place that they have no time to enter the world of their people.

"Many pastors are so busy maintaining the fourth place that they have no time to enter the world of their people."

Yet sadly, this is exactly what people are longing for. I hear the same cry from people, especially millennials, all the time:

Know me as an individual.

Stop preaching at me as if my life is the same as everyone else's in this room.

Help me explore my questions.

Help me connect my faith to the reality of school shootings, Muslim extremism, LGBTQ, the environment and politics.[47]

Do you hear what people are saying? *Stop expecting me to volunteer in your fourth place world if you refuse to take any interest in my world!* Ironically, what our people are longing for is exactly what Jesus modeled.

A Biblical Pastor

One day there was a young man named Simon in his boat fixing his nets after catching nothing all night. He was exhausted and probably a little angry and bitter about how life was turning out. A rabbi was teaching nearby, but Simon stayed in his boat. Maybe he thought the rabbi wanted nothing to do with him because he had a big mouth and a pattern of getting himself into trouble. Regardless, the rabbi came over and asked to borrow Simon's boat. He even let Simon stay with him as he started to teach the people on shore. Crazy enough, once he was done teaching, the rabbi wanted to spend more time one-on-one with Simon. He had him push off into deeper water and they had a conversation that would change Simon's destiny forever.

You know the rest of the story; Simon becomes Peter. It started because Jesus entered Simon's world. Jesus wasn't afraid to get his hands dirty with some fishermen. He didn't call Peter off to some building where

---

[47] For more research and experience with millennial opinions about church, see Sam Eaton's, "12 Reasons Millenials Are OVER Church," http://tosavealife.com/faith/12-reasons-millennials-church/, April 25, 2017.

he would train him how to become a famous orator. No, for three years he trained Simon how to see God's kingdom come to life right within his world.

After the resurrection, Peter went back to fishing and, once again, Jesus came to Peter's shore. After some breakfast, Jesus looked into Peter's eyes and said, "Feed my sheep" (John 21:17). The word *pastor* literally means *shepherd* in the original Greek. When Jesus told Peter to feed his sheep he was calling him to pastor his church—to shepherd his flock. Jesus trained Peter how to be a pastor and it had nothing to do with **a holy person doing holy things in a holy place.**

We have to assume that when Jesus said to Peter, "Feed my sheep," that Jesus implied, "Do what I've been doing with you." Peter would not have heard Jesus say, "Feed my sheep" and assumed that he really meant, "Hole up in a building and preach once a week. Use the building as your office. Do some weddings and funerals." For Jesus, pastoring his flock was about shepherding souls right within their world. It was about growing seeds into mature plants. It was about seeing the kingdom vision realized in a human life.

In John 4, Jesus entered the world of the Samaritans. He met a woman in a *third place,* at a well. He built a relationship. He planted a seed. This relationship opened the door to the rest of the town of Sychar. Jesus was invited to their *first places,* their homes and tables. His disciples witnessed it all. Jesus took them with him everywhere he went and modeled how to live. In the midst of this racism-shattering experience he looked at them and talked about the harvest being plentiful but the workers being few. Then he sent them out two by two. To do what? To do the things he had been modeling. While he was planting a new seed in the woman at the well he was maturing his disciples into trees that would bear more fruit.

Now this will sound absurd, but imagine for a minute that Jesus stopped his whole discipleship "enter their world" thing and instead he did what we do. Instead of integrating with the people, Jesus built a Jewish synagogue in Samaritan Sychar. He built a reader board out front saying, "Wells aren't the only place to find living water." Then he sat in his synagogue office all day in the event that some Sycharian actually showed up for a hand out or some counseling. He planned sermons, paid the bills, and responded to some nasty letters. Then he coordinated his Jewish leaders for the weekend service and some outreach events.

If this sounds ridiculous painting Jesus with our own pastor brush, then why is it so normal for us? Sadly, our working definition of the word *pastor* is formed out of Constantine's church, not the life of Jesus. Many aspects of our pastoral job description are simply not biblical. The great tragedy is that while many of our leaders become holy celebrity personas, the rest of us are getting smaller.

While modern technology gives us immediate access to some of the biggest Christian superstars in history, we also have a largely biblically illiterate church. We are downloading millions of sermon podcasts while many people in our churches are afraid to have a spiritual conversation with their neighbors. They are convinced they could never speak to a nonbeliever with the same knowledge or authority of their pastor. We have outsourced ministry to the professionals and it is stunting our growth.

Parenting 101

Parenting 101 states that if you want your kids to stay emotional babies their entire life, keep spoon feeding them as long as you can. Don't give them any real responsibility. Don't let them bump their head on the table. Protect them. Coddle them. Be their continual source of food and nourishment. Do this with your kids and you are sure to destroy them.

Unfortunately, we have a church culture of consumers crying out, "Feed me, feed me!" and expecting to be bottle-fed well into their old age. All blame goes toward the platform.

In 1 Corinthians, Paul accused the church of being spiritual infants because they were still fighting about their favorite teachers (1 Cor. 3:1-4). Ironically, Paul's accusation of infancy had nothing to do with the quality of teaching, nor the competency of the teachers, but instead the needy and critical posture of the listeners. Imagine, the teachers they were comparing were Paul, Apollos and Peter!

People who are ready for spiritual "meat" show that they have grown up by being less dependent on their parents for food. They have learned to self-feed. They are beginning to feed others. People who are arguing about the "deepest" teaching simply prove by their posture of pastoral dependency that they are not yet self-sustaining adults.

Perhaps we are thinking wrongly about our food. After talking with the woman at the well, Jesus' disciples tried to get him to go into town and get something to eat. His response in John 4:34: "'My food,' said Jesus, 'is to do the will of him who sent me and to finish his work.'" Jesus was fed as he actively went about his Father's business. Maybe it is time to challenge the long-held assumption that if we just preach the right sermons our people are sure to grow.

Sermons Are Not Enough

I remember one meeting with a church consultant where he asked our pastor, "What is your plan to grow your people this year?" The pastor quickly got out his preaching calendar and started talking about his various sermon series. The consultant asked, "Where's the other half?" The pastor asked, "What do you mean, 'the other half'?" The consultant replied, "I mean the systems you need in place so that people can actually do the stuff you are telling them to do."

Sermons alone are simply not enough for people to grow up in Christ. Let's look at Jesus' pattern for growing people. He invited ordinary people to join his spiritual family on mission together. He modeled and taught them how to do the mission. He empowered them to do it while he watched and debriefed. Then he released them to reproduce more disciples.

Jesus' spiritual growth pattern matches normal human development. As children grow we give them some responsibility, small at first. We empower them to test out their own wings in the world. We teach them how to drive with a permit, and then they are ready on their own. We send them to college or to the workplace. They usually return home for awhile. We debrief. We discuss. We send them out again. Eventually, they figure out how to provide for themselves, maybe even have some children of their own, then repeat the process.

Dr. Henry Cloud and Dr. John Townsend in their book, *How People Grow*, list multiple factors for spiritual growth. For them, the big picture of growth is returning to our original created intent in the garden. This not only involves a restored relationship to God, but also life-giving human relationships, meaningful work in the world and more.[48] This process of restoration involves acceptance, forgiveness, suffering, discipline, obedience and authentic community.

There is so much more to growth than lecture-based learning environments. Businesses and the education system are realizing this, yet churches seem to be the last to catch on. My close friend Tim works for Starbucks and oversees a team responsible for operational efficiency in thousands of stores. He told me that in order to create dedicated and successful partners (employees), Starbucks utilizes a training model of

---

[48] Dr. Henry Cloud and Dr. John Townsend, *How People Grow* (Grand Rapids: Zondervan, 2001), 27.

70 percent on-the-job training, 20 percent mentoring relationships and 10 percent instructional content.

What if we applied the Starbucks 70/20/10 plan to your church? How much of your church discipleship strategy is on-the-job training? Mentoring? Content delivery? If your church is like most modern churches, I bet its highest percentage is spent on content delivery.

I'm not saying that Starbucks should dictate our discipleship process, but when we think of the life of Jesus, "on-the-job training" makes a lot of sense. We can picture it. We know how Jesus trained his disciples as they traveled along the way. We may even be able to picture it when we think about InterVarsity and other parachurch ministries that spend their time in this region:

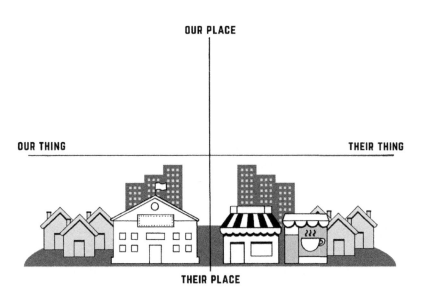

InterVarsity trains leaders by teaming them up in college dorms with more experienced leaders. The students learn how to disciple by watching others do it and participating in it. Inviting. Modeling. Empowering. Releasing.

A Different Kind of Church
by Dudley Callison

I took a group of financial partners to visit one of our churches in Europe. This church is embedded deeply within a city that is home to many North African immigrants. Before the trip, these friends posed all the "right" questions: "Will we be there for the church service and hear the sermon? Can we attend a Bible study? When will we get to join them in local evangelism efforts?" My only response was, "You'll just have to wait to see."

When we arrived, the leaders introduced us to their way of being the church. Their fellowship centered on caring for immigrant children and families. The after-school program has become known throughout the city as an effective means of integration, language and culture learning, and academic success. Without apology, the leaders describe their approach as based on the life and teachings of Jesus Christ.

As we participated one afternoon, a teenage girl shared that she was having disturbing dreams, full of fear. We watched as one of the leaders entered into that conversation with her and helped her find peace and comfort in Jesus. Evangelism unfolded before our eyes. The next day we took twenty kids to the local tree-top ropes course. The leader prayed for the group, not just for safety, but for discovery of courage and Jesus as the source of it. The experienced kids became the "disciplers," showing the new kids how to face their fears and overcome them by faith. As our trip wrapped up, my friends had not yet attended a traditional church service or heard a sermon from a pulpit. But their overwhelming response was, "Thank you for taking us to church. We never knew it could be like this."

InterVarsity's vision statement is "To see students and faculty transformed, campuses renewed, and world changers developed." They realize this vision by coming alongside students in their world, not asking them to leave their world and sit in a *fourth place*.

Yet most of our "local" churches largely have growth backward. We are trying to grow people using Constantine's forms, yet those forms were designed to keep people reliant on a holy celebrity persona.

Adults who stay dependent on their parents for life have issues often requiring counseling. Yet that is what we have in our churches—a fee-for-service financial model where people think they are tithing in order to pay for good spiritual food from the pastor. Is it any wonder congregants whine and complain when their food isn't made to order? Now pastors are the ones in counseling, wondering why they are working so hard and seeing so little growth.

A Place for Preaching

If you are concerned that I want us all to do away with preaching, that is not what I am saying. Jesus often preached to large crowds, as did the apostles. Clearly preaching is biblical and is a key component in any church. The problem isn't preaching; it is the absolute dominance of preaching in the overall discipleship strategy of the local church.

Willow Creek, one of the largest evangelical churches in the country, conducted a study called Reveal where they surveyed over 250,000 people in more than 1,000 churches across many denominations. They broke down the spiritual journey into four segments: *Exploring Christ*, *Growing in Christ*, *Close to Christ* and *Christ Centered*. They evaluated the most effective ways of helping people move from one segment to the next. Preaching and worship services were found to be helpful for the first movement—from *Exploring Christ* to *Growing in Christ*.

According to *Move*, the book describing the survey results, "Weekend services most benefit those in the earliest stages."[49]

Biblically this make sense. Paul asks, "How will they believe unless they hear?" Clearly there is a part of the growth continuum that does require some spoon-feeding. There is a point at which people actually *are* spiritual infants. As people moved down the continuum, Willow Creek found that it was personal spiritual practices, especially personal Bible reading, that was by far the most important factor in growth. In other words, people moved from depending on the pastor for food to self-feeding as they became spiritual adults.

As the church in the West, we are buying into a dangerous misconception as to our source of food. We have a church culture so accustomed to a steady overfeeding diet of sermons that churchgoers are no longer hungry. Knowledgeable Christians are stalling out in their growth and becoming critics while they should be moving onto self-feeding and spiritual reproduction.

Preaching has an important place, but it is not our primary means of growth. The pastor's role is not merely to feed the already satiated, but to cultivate spiritual hunger and a culture of self-feeding. Growth requires a community of mutual participation, not a room designed for a celebrity and their adoring fans. Many evangelical Christians are now looking to the spiritual formation movement for real growth. Sunday morning is simply not feeding their souls anymore. Jesus' pastors were shepherds of spiritual families; our pastors end up shepherds of spiritual events. There is a big difference. The spiritual formation movement is not rooted in Constantine's events, but in the monastic life of spiritual

---

[49] Greg L. Hawkins and Cally Parkinson, *Move* (Grand Rapids: Zondervan, 2011), 115.

family. The resources come not from the medium of the stage, but from lives of deep prayer, contemplation, shared community and suffering.

The medium is the message, right now our preacher-centric structures are designed to make holy celebrity personas and small dependent Christians. The stage-based pastoral job description is not working.

Where Are We Going?

As with the last chapter on **place**, this chapter on **people** is pushing on some long-held views of who pastors are and what they should do. For some, you agree that we have a major issue with our pastoral job description, but you are not sure what the alternative might be.

Don't worry, as much as we have described the negative fruit of the **separation** of clergy and laity, we will talk about the wonderful possibilities of **integration** in Chapter 10. We will tell the stories of many churches using a fundamentally different leadership model and what that can look like.

Plus, we have only really talked about pastors in this chapter. Why? Because that is the only gift we really affirm and pay for in the West. We will see in Chapter 10 that redefining the role of the pastor allows for the possibility to utilize the other gifts of apostles, prophets, evangelists and teachers (Eph. 4:11). Not only that, it will also allow pastors to finally be pastors, shepherds of people, rather than *fourth place* event planners.

Where Are You?

In the last chapter, you identified your building on the chart. That was just the first step of evaluating your church media. Now we need to identify where you are in terms of the medium of **people**. Why? Because it is possible to practice **integration** in one medium, yet practice

separation in another medium. For example, if you meet in a concert venue or school, yet your whole church culture still revolves around a weekend service with a big personality, then you have integrated **place**, but not **people**.

Integrating **people** means that you have a church culture of mutual participation where every voice and gift matters. These gifts are not primarily used to run *fourth places*. Instead, your church is designed to walk with and empower people as they learn to enjoy God's presence and use their gifts in their world.

So, where are you?

OUR THING, OUR PLACE

If your church revolves around the *fourth place* event and there are usually one or two main voices on stage, you would likely identify yourself in OUR THING, OUR PLACE. You would also be here if staff time, stress and budget primarily revolve around getting people to run your *fourth place* events and programs.

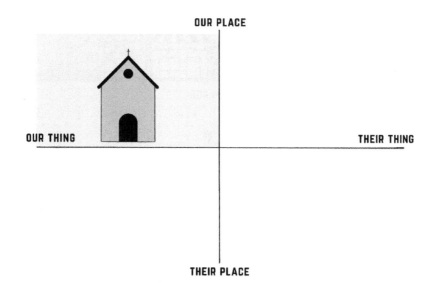

OUR THING, THEIR PLACE

If you have empowered a second tier of unpaid leaders who are leading small groups or missional communities within culturally relevant spaces, you have moved into the OUR THING, THEIR PLACE quadrant. If small groups are little more than your organization's way to grow your *fourth place*, you are still in the top part of this grey area; however, if your church has given legitimate pastoral responsibility to these leaders and you view these gatherings as equally part of your definition of "church," then you have moved toward a more integrated approach to **people**.

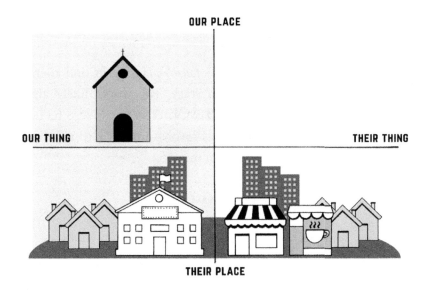

THEIR THING, OUR PLACE

Perhaps you own a building and are able to use it to bring the world to you. Maybe one of your staff members, instead of sitting in her office, runs a public coffee shop or coworking business right from your facility. If your job involves tenant relationships, small business, or running a concert venue, you might be somewhere in this region:

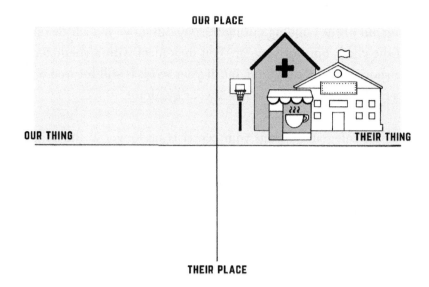

THEIR THING, THEIR PLACE

To the degree that your church's ministry involves living and working alongside normal humans you have moved into the THEIR THING, THEIR PLACE quadrant.

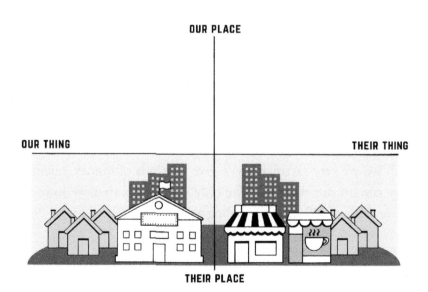

Getting out of the building during the day can move you a little further down the chart, but not very far. You may meet with a volunteer in a coffee shop from time to time, but if your work is still focused on the events of the *fourth place*, that is still your quadrant.

To be fully integrated means your center is no longer in the building. Think of an InterVarsity Director. They office at the coffee shop. They hang out on campus. They go to the football game. Where is their center? Their center is as mobile as the people they are trying to love and disciple. If your leadership job descriptions are designed around walking with people in the context of their normal life, helping them to see Christ's kingdom vision realized in their world, put your church somewhere in this region.

Where are you? Go ahead and make an "X" on the graphic above to indicate your starting point in terms of the medium of **people**.

One More Medium

We are now two-thirds of the way toward understanding Constantine's impact on the church. We have seen that not only did Constantine move the church into the *fourth place*, but that this move had a major impact on the way we view and approach Christian leadership.

We have one more medium to address, our **practices**. Paul urged believers, "Offer your bodies as living sacrifices" (Rom. 12:1). As a church we are very sacrificial. We give all kinds of money, talent and energy toward our worship. The only problem is that we have been offering those sacrifices at the wrong altar.

7

A Misplaced Sacrifice

R ecently I had the privilege of attending my first grade son's Veterans Day program. We met in the school cafeteria. The kids sang the classic patriotic songs and did choreographed motions. During another portion of the program, a dad serving as a major in the Army showed a slide show of his experience in Iraq.

The production quality of the event was what you'd expect from a first grade cafeteria performance. The transitions were awkward. There was dead space everywhere. When the projection screen scrolled down from the ceiling, it sounded like a dying witch. The volume for the "multimedia" presentation (a YouTube video) wasn't working. One kid showed up late and took at least a minute to squirm past fifteen other kids on the risers. The crowd let out an audible sigh of relief when she was finally situated.

There was nothing remarkable about the production quality. Yet when the major talked about parting from his son for fifteen months, there was not a dry eye in the room. He closed with this quote from GK

Chesterton: "The true soldier fights not because he hates what is in front of him, but because he loves what is behind him." More tears.

It was not an *excellent* performance, yet all the people I talked to afterward said it was the best Veterans Day celebration they had ever experienced. I agreed with them. How could it be the best celebration, yet lack all modern production standards? Poor timing. Poor sound equipment. Average speaking. Kids picking their noses and missing cues. What about an elementary school Veterans Day performance makes it so professional men and women can come, be deeply touched, and have no concern for quality? Conversely, what is it about the church that we can invest countless dollars and hours into a special church service and people still walk away as critics? Where is the disconnect?

I want to suggest that the disconnect has to do with a misplaced sacrifice. When Constantine made church an event in a building, the location of our sacrifice changed. While Jesus and the early church sacrificed themselves for each other and their world, many of us are now giving our lives in order to run events in our *fourth places* (our church buildings).

To carry our Veterans Day analogy a step further, the major talking at the assembly didn't care about production quality because he knew that his real battlefield was not in that cafeteria. As a church, our time, energy and resources go primarily toward worship services in buildings because we consider our services the battlefield. We have misplaced our sacrifice. We are sacrificing on the wrong altar.

In our journey of church forms, we have discussed **place** and **people**, and now we come to our final form, **practices**. When Constantine and Christendom moved the church into the *fourth place*, Christian practices made a fundamental shift. The rhythms of Christianity, rather than revolving primarily around a shared life in community, began to revolve around buildings and programs.

What is the impact of Christendom on our **practices**? In short, we became very good at all the wrong things. We will see in this chapter that we are now running a version of Christianity that takes a great deal of money and effort, yet isn't designed to actually grow people to live and act like Jesus in the world.

God Loves Excellence

There is a popular myth in the church and it goes something like this: "God loves excellence, so everything we do should be done with excellence." Ask any worship leader why the music must be great and the answer will likely be, "God loves excellence." Ask the production manager why they need such elaborate stage design. "God loves excellence."

They may quote Romans 12:1 and tell you that worship is a sacrifice. If that's the case, then the quality of our sacrifice matters. After all, Leviticus 22:21 says, "When anyone brings from the herd or flock a fellowship offering to the Lord to fulfill a special vow or as a freewill offering, it must be without defect or blemish to be acceptable." Don't we want to be acceptable to God?

Verses like these can lead us to believe that we need to offer our sacrifices without any blemish or defect. If worship is our sacrifice, then it follows that our productions should be free of blemishes or defects. We should work hard and spend whatever resources it takes to get the best sound, the best musicians, the best lighting. After all, God loves excellence and God deserves our very best, right? Maybe not.

God does love excellence, but only in the right things. A person can be an excellent drug dealer or con-artist. We can't assume that just because we *do* something, that God wants us to do that thing really well. It is the *object* of excellence that matters, not excellence at *all* things.

Consider Paul's words in Philippians 4:8: "...whatever is excellent, think about such things." Here, Paul does NOT state that we should do everything with excellence. On the contrary, he says that some things are excellent and some things are not. We should think about the things that really *are* excellent, not the other things. The more important question to ask then is, "What does God think is excellent?"

Many of us have simply assumed that since we have grown up with worship services at the center of the church experience that God must be really interested in worship service excellence. The only problem is, this assumption is not what the Bible teaches, nor what Jesus and the early church modeled.

Worship as Life

If God is not looking for great worship services, then what is he looking for? We will discuss this much more in the next chapter. In summary, we were created in the garden to experience all of life as worship to God—*the everywhere worship of Eden*. Prior to the fall and the need for a temple, worship revolved around relationship.

With God.
With each other.
With the creation itself.

We were designed to be stewards of God's creation. Created in the image of God, we were to live in such a way that our life on earth reflected his love and justice. Worship and life were one. When our connection to God was lost, he gave us the physical temple building and its sacrificial system. This was temporary. Jesus' coming moved the temple out of the building and into a human being. Friends, Jesus did not leave heaven and come to earth just to help us rebuild temples and write hit worship tunes. No, he had something much bigger in mind.

"Jesus did not leave heaven and come to earth just to help us rebuild temples and write hit worship tunes."

His coming moved worship from here to here:

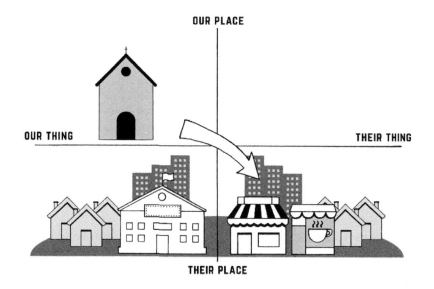

This is the point of the incarnation. Everything about worship, **place (temple)**, **people (priest)** and **practices (sacrifice)**, all became embodied in a Jewish man from Nazareth. The entire system of worship moved back into the neighborhood.

What Christ modeled, we are to continue today as his body.

The New Testament shows a progression from the building back into reality. Paul's life became the "drink offering" (2 Tim. 4:6). Hebrews takes the altar "outside the camp" and describes the "sacrifice" as taking care of people with needs (Heb. 13:10-16). We even see the Levitical instructions about blemishes reimagined. Paul writes, "But now he has reconciled you by Christ's physical body through death to present you holy in his sight, without blemish and free from accusation" (Col. 1:22).

Did you catch that? It's not our guitar solos and stage lighting that should be without blemish, it's us! Not because we wear stage makeup, but because we are a forgiven people and now stand blemish-free before God.

When Jesus looked into the eyes of the woman at the well, he saw every blemish of her past. He also saw something else—a child of God with a story about to be redeemed. He saw a life capable of carrying the good news about Jesus into her culture like none of his male Jewish disciples ever could. He saw the future of worship—not a bunch of Samaritans needing to become like Jews in order to worship God at their temple, rather a new breed of worshipers who would be full of the Spirit of God, ready to be released to redeem Sychar from within.

Our modern worship that draws people out of their culture and into our Christian subculture is not the worship Jesus came to give us. *Fourth place* worship **separates** us from our world. Jesus' worship **integrates** us back into it.

Mercy Is Our Sacrifice

Confusion about worship excellence is nothing new. The religious leaders in Jesus' day were also overly obsessed with temple excellence. Remember the story of Matthew's party of "sinners" when all the religious leaders showed up? The Pharisees could not comprehend someone who claimed to be a Jewish rabbi purposefully eating and drinking with the filth of the earth. Temple "excellence" required staying ceremonially clean. To them that meant avoiding dirty people.

Jesus rebuked them, saying, "I desire mercy, not sacrifice" (Matt. 9:13). Mercy, NOT sacrifice. In other words, I'm more concerned with these beautiful sinful people than with your temple "excellence."

For the Pharisees, mercy and sacrifice were both good things. The religious leaders were not being disobedient when they cared about the quality of their temple sacrifices. Sacrificial excellence was commanded by God in the law; however, God has an opinion as to what matters more, and his priority has always been mercy. This was not only true in the New Testament, but also the Old Testament. Hosea 6:6 states, "For I desire mercy, not sacrifice, and acknowledgment of God rather than burnt offerings."

Mercy has always been superior to sacrifice, but for the Jewish people, temple sacrifices were also important. Jesus himself represented this tension. Jesus was consumed by mercy, but he was also an observant Jew. He practiced both justice for the outsider as well as the liturgy of the insider. Jesus never condemned the temple nor the temple sacrifices. He participated in them because he represented the overlap of the ages—a human temple attending a physical temple.

What about us? We are no longer required to offer temple sacrifices; we should be free to give our undivided attention and resources to mercy. For us, mercy *is* the sacrifice. This is not just good theory or rhetoric; this is how the early church actually practiced their faith. Look at how Justin Martyr's community from around 150 AD used their resources:

> What is collected is deposited with the overseer. He uses it for the care of orphans and widows, for those who are suffering want arising from illness or any other cause, for

prisoners, and for travelers staying with us for a short time. Briefly, he provides for all who are in need in the town.[50]

What percentage of your church budget goes toward running the physical temple and what portion goes toward compassion for the human temples in your community?

Worship for Justin no longer had to do with temple excellence but with sacrificial living for each other. Justin's church was a community of mercy. If we are ever going to be able to reprioritize our churches around mercy rather than temple excellence, we are going to need to put our sacrifice back where it belongs—back into real life.

Families and Weddings

By the front door in my home, there's a sign that says, "Enjoy the little things in life, for one day you will look back and realize they were the big things." The real substance of family is in the "little things"—work, play, fighting, making-up, kids, conversations, eating, messes, sleep, love, serving neighbors, enjoying friends and sports—the normal, the everyday. The basic family gathering happens around the dinner table. We pray, eat and talk about what's going on in life. There's some drama—a kid won't eat, a high schooler had a bad day at school, work was rough for Mom or Dad. But everything is okay—we're together now eating a meal. It's informal and casual. There's good food and good drink. People can be themselves and let their guard down.

These are normal family rhythms—family **practices**—the "little things." Occasionally we do a "big thing"—a family vacation, an

---

[50] Justin Martyr, "First Apology," lxvii, in Eberhard Arnold, *The Early Christians in Their Own Words*, 250.

elaborate birthday party, an anniversary. And of course there is the biggest day of them all, the wedding.

Weddings are big events. You hire a wedding planner and spend a ton of money. You dress up, and your family members become your volunteer ushers and greeters. Uncle Larry sings a solo. Little Danny is the ring bearer. The event is formal. If a transition goes bad, it's awkward. Everyone is exhausted when it's all over, but that's okay. You did it together, and it was beautiful. Stressful, but beautiful. And you won't have to do it again for another couple of years.

Now imagine a family who decides to stop having family meals together. In fact, they also decide to stop living together. Rather than experiencing everyday life together, they only come together every weekend for a wedding. No more "little things," just the "big things." Over and over, every weekend.

You might be thinking, who in their right mind would do that? Who would trade the real substance, variety and authenticity of family for a life of stressful weekend events? Sound familiar? In general, our modern church services have all of the elements of a formal wedding plus some extras. People get dressed up, and professionals run the production. We need ushers, greeters, programs, parking lot attendants, sound systems, video producers, trained vocalists, professional orators and well-timed transitions.

Why are we doing this? Because of Constantine's foundational paradigm: **Church is primarily an event in a building.** Somewhere along the way, church changed from a community of mostly "little things" to a weekly wedding ceremony. We started sacrificing ourselves on the altar of the *fourth place.*

Justin, Tertullian, Paul, Peter, Jesus and the rest based their gatherings around the rhythms of the family meal, not the family wedding. At a meal, the social rules are different. Nobody cares about perfect timing, production quality or flawless public speaking. People are too busy enjoying themselves around good food and conversation to care. If someone messes up dinner, you don't simply leave. You are connected by a relationship, not a performance.

Some of you may be thinking, "That's just because the church was small. You can't have an informal meal at a megachurch of ten thousand." This is a good observation, but it is actually thinking about the issue backwards. Many of us think of church as the event and small groups as an optional place for people to experience life together. This is backwards. The primary definition of church is the spiritual family. All families need the "little things." The optional part is actually the "big things."

Jesus took a common meal with common people and made it sacred. This is significant because *the medium is the message.* By making a common meal holy, the gathering reflected the nature of Jesus himself. What does that mean?

The common meal represents the message of the gospel. The gospel was not just what Jesus said with his mouth; it was proclaimed by his very nature. Jesus is the word of God—God expressed as a medium. When God wanted to build a bridge back to humanity, it is significant that he didn't send a rock star but instead he sent a vulnerable baby. God wanted us to know that he accepts us in our weakness. He accepts the common, not just the spectacular. That's why the medium of our gathering matters. When we eat common food with common people we are reminded that God still saves sinners. Romans 5:8 tells us, "But God demonstrates his own love for us in this: While we were still sinners, Christ died for us." Not when we clean ourselves up or get every note right. While we were still sinners.

We have seen that our current way of practicing church is expensive and time-consuming. That is a big problem. But a much deeper problem is that when we put professional polish on our gatherings we no longer reflect the nature of Jesus. Instead of reflecting a gospel for the broken, we are actually reflecting the message of legalism—the notion that in order to get to God we need to clean ourselves up enough to be presentable. In doing so, we reflect every other religion in the world that has to work to appease its God. Our striving after performance excellence, though cloaked in the language of biblical sacrifice, is actually an assault on the gospel itself.

Think about the mixed messages we are sending people all the time. We preach about grace, all the while trying to deliver a sermon without mistakes. We put the beautiful and talented on stage, all the while telling our little girls not to worry about their body image.

Trying to be vulnerable and authentic every week on stage is about as effective as taking children to the mall in December and telling them to focus on "the real meaning of Christmas." Our "weddings" aren't allowing us to be sinners saved by grace. They are forcing us to be performance-oriented imposters. We can't help ourselves because we're on a stage and we underestimate the power of our medium. We know we are supposed to be a safe family where people can be themselves, but the best we can muster is a staged family photo shoot where everyone has to pretend to have it all together. We are a photoshopped church, but the gospel is about the genuineness of the candid moment.

"We are a photoshopped church, but the gospel is about the genuineness of the candid moment."

We mistakenly equate deep commitment to church with time spent running events, but Jesus really just wants us deeply committed to each other. We are sacrificing for the *fourth place* when we should be sacrificing for one another. The New Testament is ripe with commands to love one another, serve one another, encourage one another and submit to one another. There is not a single command to perform church services with excellence.

A.W. Tozer explains our reality like this:

> Right now we are in an age of religious complexity. The simplicity which is in Christ is rarely found among us. In its stead are programs, methods, organizations and a world of nervous activities which occupy time and attention but can never satisfy the longing of the heart. The shallowness of our inner experience, the hollowness of our worship, and that servile imitation of the world which marks our promotional methods all testify that we, in this day, know God only imperfectly, and the peace of God scarcely at all.[51]

And he was writing in 1949. Before megachurches.

Some of you may be thinking, "Can't we just do what a lot of megachurches do—weekly 'big thing' events AND really good 'little thing' small groups?" This is a great question and one I have spent a lot of time processing for myself. I personally spent three years pastoring small groups at a megachurch.

Here is the problem with this solution. If it is true that our performance-oriented excellence is built on the medium of legalism,

---

[51]A.W. Tozer, *The Pursuit of God* (Camp Hill: Christian Publications; 1993), 17-18.

then this is a poison to be avoided, not an ingredient to keep in a well-balanced diet. To do both small groups and large production is to say, "I want a nice blend in my medium of some gospel and some religious performance." Some sinner saved by grace and some good self-improvement show.

This is why I eventually needed to leave the megachurch even though I loved my church, our worship leaders, and my role of helping people find community in small groups. I realized we were not maintaining a balance of large and small. Rather, we were maintaining a balance of gospel and legalism. Freedom and works.

I understand this might be difficult to hear, but it is true. It has to be true. The medium of Jesus has to matter. God identified himself among the dirty shepherds, sinners, tax collectors and prostitutes. God didn't hire talent, but common fishermen.

If our platforms are only accessible to the strong and talented, the polished and clean, we have rebuilt Christendom's screens and simply given them a new name: the stage.

And let's not pretend performance excellence is just an issue in the megachurch. No, in fact, it's usually just that megachurches are performing better and the rest of us are working harder with less resources in order to keep up.

Now I want to be clear. Large gatherings are possible. Large churches are possible. I am not simply advocating house church here. There are many other options. We will talk about all of this. Not every wedding is a performance. You can gather with a large group of people and not need a big show. You can gather in a large building and not create a new holy place. We need to sing, and pray and experience God up close and personal. I'm not suggesting we stop these practices. I'm suggesting there is a better way to practice church that doesn't depend on performance. I have personally felt close to God in a Hillsong United concert. I have also encountered God on a rickety old bus driving the streets of Nicaragua, singing songs of praise with my friends on a cross-cultural trip. God has never cared about performance or size or cost. He cares about the heart.

Why the Tears?
by Dudley Callison

I was surprised by the tears that flowed as I worshipped at our Communitas staff conference. These are the same songs we sing at the megachurch back home. Why the tears now? Back home we have pro-grade musicians, everything you could want from a sound system, lighting and stage design. Don't you get what you pay for? Shouldn't the extra money and effort make weekly corporate worship more meaningful? Then why do I find myself in that environment singing blandly and looking around, somewhat disconnected from God?

Then it struck me—at the staff conference I was surrounded by people I know and love, the people I serve alongside. I realized once again that worship isn't about all of the bells and whistles, but about a community engaged with God together in life and mission. I'm sure the strangers standing near me back home also love Jesus and may even participate in extending God's love to others, but they are not part of my community. We don't participate together in mission. We don't sacrifice for each other. We don't fight together to love our neighborhood. You simply cannot separate worship from community. You can't separate worship from mission. No dollar amount can replace the presence of God alive and active in a community that loves each other and serves together.

The sad reality is that for all of our sincere effort and our millions of dollars, our performance-oriented version of excellence is putting us in a position where we are actually doing the exact opposite of what people need in order to become more like Jesus.

We have misplaced our sacrifice. We are like a couple who put all of their life savings into the wedding but forgot to plan for the marriage.

Discipleship Confusion

The Western church has largely bought into the myth that says, "If we can just get our weekend services right, then somehow people will meet Jesus and become disciples." We discussed in the last chapter how this myth impacts our view of preaching. We think that preaching great sermons will somehow translate into spiritual growth, when in fact, dependence on our preachers for our "food" keeps us spiritual infants.

The same myth impacts our worship. We seem to think that if we can get the right gear, the right worship leader, the right style of music or the perfect gospel-shaped liturgy, then people will finally encounter God and become disciples. Unfortunately, this myth is reiterated in much of the literature on worship.

Jesus took twelve men with him not into the temple, but into life's trenches. He gave them a real meal around a table that forced them to look at each other and actually talk to one another. It's not about perfecting the liturgy of our services, it's about getting the liturgy out of the *fourth place*. Confession makes sense in community; it doesn't make much sense sitting alone in a pew. Communion works around a table. It reflects the reality that we are all broken yet can maintain relationship because we have a great savior. But make it a moment of silence with a stale cracker and a tiny plastic shot glass and you lose more than the fun of a good meal, you lose the gospel.

Does that mean we should never have any quality services or excellent music? It depends if you are starting a church "from scratch" or from an existing system. At a minimum, it means that "excellent" services are not necessary and are sometimes harmful. If you are starting from a building-centered paradigm, maybe you need to think about how often your community needs their "weddings" and how often they need "meals." It may be time to check the balance.

Again, there is a lot we can learn from the parachurch. Young Life, for example, runs camps with a high degree of performance excellence, but kids don't go to camp every week, they do it once or twice a year. During the weeks and months they are not at camp, kids are discipled in Campaigner Groups where they have a dialogue about their faith in a warm home. Many churches are exploring with ideas around canceling services and doing service projects instead.

I'm not anti-worship-service. God does great things through worship services. God uses every wineskin we offer to him; however, if we are honest, most of us will admit that our current wineskin is not doing a very good job making disciples. We are throwing everything we have at better worship services, promising people that serving at our churches will help them grow, and yet we continue to complain about churchgoers having a consumer mindset.

I recently had a conversation with a friend who has been volunteering as a drummer for his church for years. He wanted to talk because he didn't feel like drumming anymore, felt spiritually dry, and wanted to figure out what was wrong. As we talked, he revealed that church hadn't really felt like a spiritual family to him since his high school youth group. He had such a profound experience back then that it kept him in church for over a decade, but over time the life had been sucked out of him by the endless onslaught of Planning Center volunteer requests, new pastor visions, and subsequent pastoral flame-outs.

I shared with him the analogy of families and weddings. He said, "Yes, that's it. I feel like a wedding singer. I show up, don't really know anybody, do my drumming job, and go home." No wonder he was feeling spiritually dry. The frantic life of running service after service was keeping him from experiencing church as a spiritual family. If we want our people to live more like Jesus, we need to reconnect church to real life.

A Lid on Growth

Janet Hagberg and Robert Guelich wrote a wonderful book called *The Critical Journey*. In it they outline a normal pathway of six stages that people walk through as they grow in God. They argue that most of our churches work best for people in stages one to three. Stage three is when you are "working for God." This is the stage where people are operating out of their natural talents. This is the gifted young preacher or the hot new worship artist.

> Life becomes a performance, an act, a play, a drama in which we are the leading persons and all goes well. We cannot be vulnerable or look weak in front of others because we would be out of control. We are angry with God inside and very fearful of being found out, so our facade is stronger than ever. We look almost perfect to those around us. We are frequently worshiped as heroes. We thrive on the audience reaction. Their applause becomes addictive. We go back for more and more. We strive so hard to be loved for what we have done rather than for who we are. We are ultimately very, very lonely people.[52]

---

[52] Janet O. Hagberg and Robert A. Guelich, *The Critical Journey: Stages in the Life of Faith* (Salem, WI: Sheffield Publishing Company, 2005), 82-83.

The high never lasts. Why? Because God wants us not to function out of our flesh but out of the Spirit. All of us, if we want to walk deeper with God, will go through what Hagberg and Guelich call *the wall*. Teresa of Avila and John of the Cross called it *the dark night of the soul*. This is a necessary path where God seems distant and we continually bump into our growing questions, our uncertainties and our failures, until we realize and accept the limit of our flesh and the sufficiency of Christ. Everyone needs to walk through this pathway if they will ever get to the later stages of growth which have to do with a mature *life of love*.

Robert Clinton's book, *The Making of a Leader,* shows a similar pathway.[53] Leaders often have early life ministry success as they operate in their natural talents. However, in order to experience spiritual power and deeper love, they must walk through *life maturing*, seasons of significant testing, suffering and personal crises.

One fundamental issue with focusing on temple excellence rather than spiritual family is that we are inadvertently putting a lid on our own spiritual growth. Our performance-driven, talent-laden churches do not allow leaders to publicly walk a road that involves weakness and surrender. Our buildings are designed to attract the masses. Our pastoral job description is designed around creating a celebrity persona. Our worship culture makes us slaves to performance excellence. How can our people, let alone our leaders, move past their talent and into a deeper life in the Spirit if they are always needing to perform for the crowds?

What people need during these phases of growth is a place to practice vulnerability. They need a supportive spiritual family and an

---

[53] Dr. Robert J. Clinton, *The Making of a Leader* (Colorado Springs: NavPress), 135.

environment that doesn't force them to perform. It is no wonder, then, that God allows church after church and leader after leader to blow up or burn out. How else is God going to actually get at our hearts if he doesn't destroy the dangerous crutches of fleshly talent we so happily lean on for success?

Think about Jesus and his companions and how different their lives were from our upward trajectory of spiritual stardom. Based on our modern definition of excellence, John the Baptist, Paul and Jesus were utter failures. John ate locusts and yelled at people. Not very good stage presence! Paul wasn't the trained orator the Corinthians were looking for. Jesus would have been terrible at keeping Twitter followers. At the height of his career even his closest friends abandoned him. His timing was terrible. His transitions, well...awkward. "Eat my flesh..." what? His wardrobe? Always dirty from the road or stained by some poor wretch's blood and sweat.

It is time to stop simply preaching about the cross and start allowing our leaders to walk the pathway of the cross. The stage is a terrible place to grow. We need to get people out of the *fourth place* and into a spiritual family where they can be safe enough in the context of relationship to fail really big and still be loved. Christian gatherings should look more like a Veterans Day assembly than the perfect wedding.

Reclaiming the Battlefield

The reason a Veterans Day assembly can get away with poor production is because we all know that the excellence is external to the performance. When you have real soldiers sacrificing real lives on a real battlefield, who cares if there is poor lighting in the cafeteria? When you have real teachers investing their lives in real kids we know and love, who cares if the kids are two full beats behind the track on "Yankee Doodle Dandy"? It doesn't matter. When you have real substance, you don't need a great show to convince people to stick around.

Friends, we have excellence completely backwards. God loves excellence in neighboring. God loves sacrificial living in the workplace. God loves long-enduring relationships. Let's reconsider our definition of success in church and be excellent in things that God cares about. It is time to put the sacrifice back where it belongs.

Where Are You?

A lot of this may be new to you. It is a paradigm shift from the way many of us have been raised to think about church. Many people, when I talk about this topic, have a guttural response that says, "But I love my worship services!" My own mother has a hard time talking about all of this. She loves high church. I get it.

Many of us have had amazing experiences in worship services. We have encountered God there. Our lives have been changed there. I am not trying to take anything away from your or my past experience. However, we have a big problem and tweaking the service isn't going to fix it.

Many of us feel stuck. If we don't perform better than the church next door, people will leave and go to that church. If we don't preach good sermons or lead quality worship we might get fired. These are very real pressures. Many pastors are struggling to keep the doors open and the last thing they want to hear is, "Stop putting all of your time and energy into your services and start loving your neighbors." Some may be thinking, "Our facility is a mess, I never have enough volunteers, and my worship leader is a train wreck. You want me to stop caring about my services?"

There is no simple solution. **Place, people** and **practices** are all intimately connected. When we put the church in the *fourth place*, it demands a certain type of leader to run it and a certain type of performance excellence to keep people happy. You can't just meet in a big auditorium with an audience expecting a good show and suddenly tell them to be okay with mediocrity. They probably *will* leave.

So what are we supposed to do?

My goal in these past three chapters has simply been to expose the impact of Constantine and Christendom on our modern church. This in no way implies that there is only one correct way to respond. Some of you are ready for radical change. The next chapters should give you a lot of practical steps to take if you truly want to live as an integrated church outside of the *fourth place*.

Some of you, however, are in a place where you can only imagine incremental change at best. That's okay. We all need to balance our responsibility to the gospel against our pastoral responsibility to make changes at a rate that won't hurt our people or ourselves. For those in this situation, the coming chapters will offer helpful incremental steps that existing churches can take to move away from temple sacrifice into a life of mercy.

The first step for any of us in knowing where to move is to know where we are starting out.

So once again let's figure out where we are in terms of our **practices**. We have already charted **place** and **people**.

To keep it simple, we will once again use the same graphic. As I walk through some of the options, figure out where you and your church experience live on the chart.

The big question we are asking for **practices** is, "Where are you investing your best time, energy and resources?"

In other words, "Where are you offering your sacrifice, your excellence?"

OUR THING, OUR PLACE

Hopefully, you get it by now. If your main efforts go toward your weekend service(s), you are here:

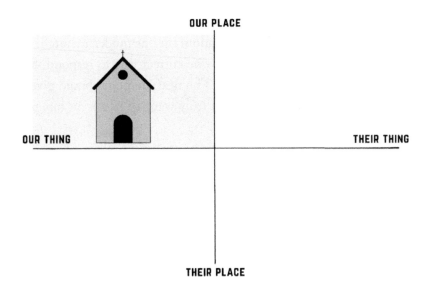

OUR THING, THEIR PLACE

If your church maintains a good balance between the large event and small groups, you are somewhere in this area. Again, it depends on your level of dependence on the religious building. Ministries like 3DM have told their missional communities to try to attend four things a month. Maybe that's three missional community gatherings and one central gathering, or maybe that's three central gatherings and one missional community. Either way, they are trying to keep real life and the *fourth place* in balance. If that's the case, your practices have moved significantly into the OUR THING, THEIR PLACE quadrant. You may still attend a large central building, but if you eat, play, sing, serve and share real life with a smaller spiritual family you have moved further down toward **integration** of **practices**.

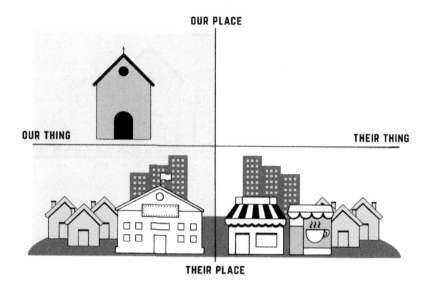

Note that simply having a small groups ministry only gets you so far. I was the Small Groups Pastor for a megachurch, and we had over one thousand people in ninety small groups. Some of these groups were sharing real life together, and many others were sparsely attended commuter groups. People were driving across the city for a nice Bible study, but there was really no shared life or mission happening. Don't assume that small groups are the whole answer if we want to integrate our churches with real life.

THEIR THING, OUR PLACE

Maybe your worship services aren't taking up all of your time and energy and instead you are putting your excellence into running legitimately cool concerts in a venue. Maybe a weekly rhythm at your church is getting your tenants together for lunch. Maybe your building is home to the Girl Scouts, AA or high school events. To the degree that your building is an excellent place for real life to happen among your neighborhood, you have moved into the THEIR THING, OUR PLACE quadrant.

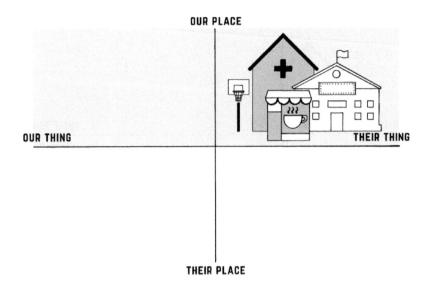

THEIR THING, THEIR PLACE

If excellent worship to you is a long walk with God and a spiritual practice for you is having a conversation with a coworker in the cubicle next to you, your **practices** are integrating with real life.

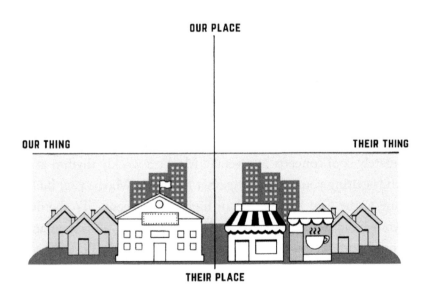

If you see parenting your kids as discipleship and mowing a neighbor's lawn with excellence as praise, you are practicing Christianity in THEIR THING, THEIR PLACE.

A bi-vocational pastor does not see their job as a hindrance but as a hub for missional activity. A Young Life Director does not see a track meet as "non-work hours" but as another opportunity to intersect with the real lives of the kids they are trying to love. To the degree that your church truly puts their time, energy and resources here, this is your quadrant.

Where are you? Go ahead and make an "X" on the graphic above to indicate your starting point in terms of the medium of **practices**.

Some of you may be wondering where the ideal church would go on the grid. Bottom right? Bottom left? A little of everything? To this point I have hinted that the bottom quadrants are where the church should reside, but I have not said it explicitly. That is because as of yet we have not talked in depth about the function of church. What is our real purpose in the world? What are we here for?

Form Follows Function

In the world of design there is a saying that *form follows function*. This little statement means that our function, or purpose, should dictate our design. Only when we know our purpose can we know where we should live on the chart.

Unfortunately, it is often the case in the church that form does NOT follow function. Our forms were designed to separate holy places from unholy places, celebrity leaders from common people, and worship personnel from the crowd. Again, it isn't that a group of people sat down and said, "How can we separate ourselves from the world and from each other? I know! We'll rebuild the temple!" Nobody says that.

We simply default to it or drift toward it over time. This is our current reality. It may feel uncomfortable or hard to accept. Many people have to move through feelings of bitterness, anger or betrayal before they can accept where we are and regain some hope for the church.

I am writing this book because I love the church. That love causes me to grieve for the church. Every day I pray and my heart hurts. I mourn over our misuse of resources. I ache for the leaders who are being destroyed and losing their faith. I am burdened for the people who aren't being spiritually fed and don't know why. Probably more than anything, I grieve over our division.

Sadly, if I'm honest, I don't see a lot of these things changing in our current design. I see little hope for unity given our attractional need to compete with one another. I heard just today of a church that has an exotic fountain that will play Christian music to a light show every fifteen minutes. While this tactic may draw a crowd from other churches, the sad truth is, this fountain is also just making sure the church sits securely divided in our separate *fourth places*.

And yet for some crazy reason, I am full of hope. Why? Because God is really big, and I'm convinced he wants to see radical change in the design of today's church. I am also convinced that this famous quote from an unknown source is true: "Every system is perfectly designed to get the results it gets."

Why does this give me hope? Because maybe our results stem from a design problem. Maybe we are living in the wrong quadrant. Maybe if we weren't designed to compete, we could see real unity take place. Maybe if we weren't designed for celebrities, we could see a network of humble leaders released into their callings. Maybe if we weren't designed around temple excellence, we could envision a church that uses its resources toward radical mercy.

We have spent the last three chapters deconstructing the church. The next section of the book moves into construction mode. As we begin to build, we'll start with the foundation by focusing on our function. We need to understand our purpose. Why do we exist? Only then will we be able to speak of the design that can best accomplish this purpose.

PART 3

OUT OF THE 4TH PLACE

8

Form Follows Function

If you are an architect in London, you do not want to win the Carbuncle Cup. This not-so-prestigious award is given to the worst building design of the year. In 2015 the award went to Rafael Vinoly, designer of the monstrosity at 20 Fenchurch Street, locally known as the "Walkie Talkie" building.[54] This thirty-seven story, bulbous-shaped student housing building is claimed to have ruined a portion of the London skyline. However, it gets much worse than merely an aesthetic eyesore. One side of the building has a concave facade that takes in sunlight and focuses an immense amount of light and heat onto a small area of the street below. The building acts as a giant magnifying glass, leading to temperatures up to 196°F (91°C) at street level. Cars and bicycles have literally melted when parked out front. There is a burn mark in the carpet of a local barber shop from the day the rug spontaneously burst into flames one hot afternoon.

---

[54] Thomas Lane, "Carbuncle Cup Winner Announced," Building Design, September 2, 2015, http://www.bdonline.co.uk/carbuncle-cup-2015-winner-announced/5077354.article#comments, accessed February 26, 2016.

The 2015 Carbuncle vote was unanimous. The "Walkie Talkie" building won by a landslide.

Design matters.

A critical concept in architecture is that **form follows function**. A building's purpose should determine its design. The function should dictate the form. If you are creating a student housing building, it should be great at housing students, not melting cars.

So it is with the church. Our forms need to follow our function. But, as we are learning, sometimes it's the other way around. Most of the time, our forms follow *precedent*. What have we done in the past? What has worked for another ministry? What does the denomination dictate? Much of that precedent was set not by Jesus, nor his apostles, nor the early church, but by a fourth century Roman emperor.

We are now entering Part 3 of the journey. We have watched in Part 1 as the mobile and living temple of Jesus was replaced by Constantine's temple of stone. We saw in Part 2 the influence of Constantine's foundations on the church of today. We have deconstructed and exposed the issues. In Part 3 it is now time to build.

In the following chapters we are going to get into the details of an integrated church design. We are going to hear the stories of churches who are living out these principles in the real world. However, to go directly to design misses the point. If we don't pause to talk seriously about the function of church, then design is simply a matter of opinion. Some might think they are succeeding at church simply because they have gathered a lot of attendees and met budget.

Without a clear definition of the purpose of church, we have no way of knowing if we are winning or losing...or melting cars.

So Many Good Options

What is the purpose of church? People answer that question in many different ways:

> *To make disciples.*
> *To save people.*
> *To love God and love each other.*
> *To serve our city.*

If you have worked in ministry any amount of time you have probably sat through many whiteboard sessions trying to come up with the perfect words to characterize the mission of your church.

Worship. Connect. Serve.
Gather. Grow. Give.

Or maybe you picked a key verse. One church chooses the great commission, "Go and make disciples" (Matt. 28:19). Another declares that Jesus came to "seek and save what was lost" (Luke 19:10). Still another espouses Jesus' mission when he unrolled the scroll and read, "The Spirit of the Lord is on me, because he has anointed me to preach good news to the poor" (Luke 4:18). Depending on which verse you chose you might think Jesus was solely about discipleship, evangelism, social justice or something else. What if Jesus cares about *all* of those things?

Start with the WHY

Let's take a step back from church and ask the same question about another type of organization. If we were looking at an NFL football team, how would we find the purpose? If we showed up to one practice we might think the goal was to push metal sleds around the grass. If we showed up to the locker room we might think the goal was to make great speeches. When we look at a complex system like a football team we can't identify the function by looking only at a few small parts. We can't start with WHAT they are doing. We need to understand WHY they are doing what they are doing. We need a bigger picture.

Simon Sinek wrote a book and gave a TED talk that went viral because it offered a very simple way for organizations to understand their purpose.[55] Sinek argues that we need to start with the WHY. Many organizations know WHAT they do or even HOW they do it, but that is not their purpose. First they need the big picture. WHY does a football team push sleds around and give speeches? They do it to win Super Bowls. At least some of them do. Others are just trying to make their owners a lot of money. Either way, the WHY dictates everything else.

Sinek maintains that you need to understand your WHY before you move onto the other two key questions, HOW and WHAT. They need to come in that order because different WHYs lead to different HOWs, which lead to different WHATs.

Football teams that want to win Super Bowls function very differently from football teams that just want to make their owners a lot of money.

1. WHY do we exist? To win Super Bowls.
2. HOW do we do it? By building a culture of excellence across the organization.
3. WHAT do we need? An excellent draft, player development program and coach.

Contrast that with an alternative version:

1. WHY do we exist? To make our owner a lot of money.

---

[55] Simon Sinek, *Start with Why* (New York: Penguin, 2009).

2. HOW do we do it? By selling a lot of tickets, merchandise and advertisements.
3. WHAT do we need? A few superstars and a great marketing team.

Do you see the distinction? Different WHYs can lead to vastly different HOWs and WHATs.

And yet most churches focus on the WHAT. We say things like, "Church is all about good preaching and worship, word and sacrament. Church exists for evangelism. Church exists for social justice." But those are the WHATs. Those are our activities. We first need to understand WHY we exist in the first place.

WHY

In order to answer WHY the church exists, we look not at the individual parts, but at the big picture. We know that Jesus is the central figure in human history, but what movement does history show revolving around that center? The overarching movement throughout history is from creation, to fall, to redemption, and finally to restoration. In short, history shows a trajectory from **separation** to **integration**.

In the fall, God's good creation was **separated** from its creator. At the end of time, we see the kingdom of God fully **integrated** with the kingdoms of the world. In the words of Habakkuk, "For the earth will be filled with the knowledge of the glory of the Lord as the waters cover the sea." How integrated are the waters and the sea? Inseparably integrated.

At the end we see Eden restored in the great garden-city. We see the end of the curse (Rev. 22:3). We see the people of God reigning on the earth just like they were created to do in the beginning (Rev. 22:5).

Only now, there is no separation. They are not just walking near God in the cool of the day (Gen. 3:8); they are one with God. This is not just a restored Eden, but a new creation where spirit and matter are one. I don't know what the specifics of this will be like. What I do know is that what has been separated will finally be fully brought back together in a beautiful unity. The integration will be complete. Those who do not know Jesus will experience complete separation, the natural result of sin.

This path from separation to integration is the course of human history. Paul, in Colossians 1:18-20, describes this process of reconciliation as the big picture of Christ's ministry:

> And he is the head of the body, the church; he is the beginning and the firstborn from among the dead, so that in everything he might have the supremacy. For God was pleased to have all his fullness dwell in him, and through him to reconcile to himself all things, whether things on earth or things in heaven, by making peace through his blood, shed on the cross.

The gospel is the proclamation that the King has returned to make all things right, to bring back together that which was separated. If we are Christ's literal body on earth, then his mission is our mission. His WHY is our WHY. The cultural mandate of Genesis to spread throughout the earth and the Great Commission of Matthew to make disciples of all nations converge into this overarching purpose: to see God's kingdom come, to see what was broken made right. Missiologist Lesslie Newbigin calls the church a "sign, instrument, and foretaste of God's redeeming grace for the whole life of society."[56] In other words, the church is supposed to be a living picture of what is to come.

---

[56] Leslie Newbigin, *The Gospel in a Pluralist Society* (Grand Rapids: Eerdmans, 1989), 232-233.

Systematic theologians agree. Wayne Grudem says, "The kingdom manifests itself through the church, and thereby the future reign of God breaks into the present...."[57] Stanley Grenz states, "The church is a dynamic reality. It consists of a people in covenant. This covenant people pioneer in the present the principles that characterize that future kingdom of God, thereby constituting a sign of the divine reign."[58] John Frame maintains, "So the church is a dynamic body, in action. It is through the church that God's kingdom comes to all the ends of the earth."[59]

Some people use different language to describe the same reality, but the big picture is clear. We are on display as a living picture of the integration to come. As we consider the design of church, then, we must keep our WHY in mind:

WHY: The church exists in order to be a living demonstration of the coming integration of all things.

Clarify the WHY

"Integration of all things" is a very broad concept. In order to make our WHY a little more specific, our second step is to clarify it a bit. Where exactly are we to demonstrate this integration?

In the famous Christmas hymn "Joy to the World," we hear the words, "He comes to make his blessings flow *far as the curse is found*." If moving from **separation** to **integration** is the overarching vision, the next question involves the extent of that separation. What exactly was

---

[57] Wayne Grudem, *Systematic Theology* (Grand Rapids: Zondervan, 1994), 864.
[58] Stanley J. Grenz, *Theology for the Community of God* (Grand Rapids: Eerdmans, 1994), 486.
[59] John Frame, *Systematic Theology: An Introduction to Christian Belief* (Phillipsburg, NJ: P&R Publishing, 2013) 1033.

separated? What needs to be reintegrated? In other words, just how far is the curse to be found?

The curse did not only affect our relationship with God. It tore a divide in all three of our primary relationships: with God, with each other, and with the creation itself.

1. We were separated from God.

Sin created a chasm between the holy and the unholy. Cherubim were set to guard the entrance of the garden. We were cut off.

2. We were separated from each other.

It was not only the marriage relationship between Adam and Eve that was broken, but all human relationships. One generation later Cain killed Abel and only several generations later God destroyed the world because of all of the violence in the time of Noah. Community was fractured. In its place came competition, personal ambition, pride and division.

3. We were separated from the creation itself.

"Cursed is the ground because of you; through painful toil you will eat of it all the days of your life" (Gen. 3:17). Our mission to fill, serve and steward the earth was tarnished. Work became toil. Resources were limited. The earth suffered drought and flood, poverty and starvation. It was a seedbed for every type of injustice.

But the gospel has far-reaching implications. The King rose from the grave to restore *all* things to God. Everything that was lost in the fall is being redeemed in Jesus—three relationships moving from **separation** to **integration**.

It is no coincidence that many church leaders and thinkers come up with lists of three things when describing their mission. Mike Breen of

3DM draws a triangle and uses the words UP, IN and OUT to describe our UPward facing relationship with God, our INward facing community relationships and our OUTward facing mission and work in the world.[60] Hugh Halter in his book, *The Tangible Kingdom,* uses the words Communion, Community and Mission.[61] Northpoint Church uses Intimacy, Community and Influence.[62] Again, the same three spheres of relationship.

> "Jesus came to heal more than just our personal sins. He came to bring peace to a world broken across three relational fault lines."

Jesus came to heal more than just our personal sins. He came to bring peace to a world broken across three relational fault lines.

If that is Jesus' mission, then that is our mission. Put these three relationships in with our WHY and we get the function of the church:

WHY (function): The church exists to be a living demonstration of integration with God, each other and our world.

Now that we have our function we can shift toward design. HOW clarifies the methods we will use to perform our function.

---

[60] Breen and Cockram, *Building a Discipling Culture.*
[61] Hugh Halter and Matt Smay, *The Tangible Kingdom* (San Francisco: Jossey-Bass, 2008), 148.
[62] "Church Overview," Northpoint Community Church, http://northpoint.org/about/ accessed March 15, 2016.

HOW

As a church, if we want to demonstrate integration to the world, there are methods that will help us and there are methods that will hurt us. Many of our church methods in the past have actually worked against our WHY. The Old Testament temple was designed around a particular WHY. The function of Israel was *one nation as a light to every nation*. Israel was supposed to shine so bright that the nations would come to their God. And that is what happened. The queen of Sheba and many others showed up to witness the wisdom of Solomon and the God of Israel.

If your WHY is *one nation as a light to every nation*, temple forms are the perfect HOW. They are great when you want to draw people to your center. The problem is, temple forms also required enculturation. The closer the nations came to the Jewish center, the more Jewish they needed to become. To come near to worship, one needed to be circumcised, learn the Jewish calendar, customs, sacrifices and rituals. To draw near to God was to become like a Jew.

That is what *fourth places* do. They extract people from their culture and usher them into a new culture. Christendom's temple forms were effective for that very purpose—they spread Roman culture across the empire. To draw near to God was to become Roman.

This is not just true historically; this is now. We have probably all seen pictures of African priests wearing English robes in the hot African sun or meeting in European buildings designed to protect against rain and snow.

And this is not just "over there." Evangelical kids are often unable to connect to the world around them because they are so deeply enculturated into the Christian entertainment and worldview of their own limited church subculture.

God's strategy with Israel, his HOW, was separation. The medium communicated a message. "Come to Israel's temple through Israel's priests in order to meet God." But that is no longer God's message. God came near. The curtain was torn. The Spirit was sent. We are no longer trying to get the nations to come to our temple to become like us. We are trying to get the temple into a world of colorful diversity. We are NOT *one nation as a light to every nation*. We are *one light for every nation*. There is a big difference. The heart is the same, but the HOW has changed.

We have a different WHY and therefore we need a different HOW. We can't demonstrate integration to the world using forms of separation. As we have seen in the past three chapters, these concepts are fundamentally at odds.

Place: A church can't exemplify integration with the city from a separate religious building.

People: A church can't demonstrate a great leveling and equality of people from a celebrity stage.

Practices: A church can't express all of life as worship when all the resources are focused on a couple of hours on Sunday.

Our method, our HOW, has been centered around a strategy of building *fourth places*, but the *fourth place* was designed for a different era, a different purpose.

It is time we integrate **place, people** and **practices**.

These concepts of **place, people** and **practices** that have framed this book correspond to the three broken relationships from the Garden of Eden that need to be reconciled.

1. HOW do we demonstrate reconciliation with God? We must integrate *place*.

Since our relationship with God was healed in Christ, we no longer need to go to a temple to meet with him. If we are going to move back toward *the everywhere worship of Eden*, it is vital that every **place** is sacred, not just the church building. Integration of **place** means that we move the church out of the *fourth place* and back into culture.

2. HOW do we demonstrate reconciliation with each other? We must integrate *people*.

Since our relationship with God was healed, we no longer need a priest to bring us to God. We all have direct access to the Father. If we are going to practice the unity of Eden, we need to reintegrate our people by reuniting clergy and laity.

3. HOW do we demonstrate reconciliation with the world? We must integrate *practices*.

Since Christ was the final sacrifice, we no longer need to focus on excellent temple worship. We need to steward our cities, our streets and our neighborhoods with justice and mercy.

Our WHY must lead to our HOW.

Here is what we have so far:

WHY: The church exists to be a living demonstration of integration with God, each other and our world.

HOW: By integrating place, people and practices.

The final question is WHAT… or is it?

The Final Question

WHAT is an important question. For most religions there is a pretty standard answer to that question. First, you make an impressive temple to let everyone know your deity is superior to the competition. Then you select a few elite people to have all of the answers and power so that the common people stay dependent. Then you create a worship system so that people can conform to your religious culture. Those are the WHATs of religion.

You start with the WHAT of **place**, the temple. You add the WHAT of **people**, the priesthood. Finally, you add the WHAT of **practices**, the worship system. The formula has worked for millennia.

Then God shocked the world.

Two thousand years ago, instead of a WHAT, God sent a WHO. He sent Jesus. God wanted a medium that could integrate with every culture of the world without destroying those cultures.

What do all cultures have in common? People. Cultures design vastly different buildings, enjoy unique styles of music and participate in a wide variety of traditions and rituals. Even so, they all have one thing in common, people.

The coming of Jesus in the incarnation marked a complete paradigm shift. When Jesus came to earth, everything that constituted the temple—the building itself, the stones, the Holy of Holies, the gates, the priest, the lampstand, the tithe, the lamb, the blood, everything— were all simultaneously present in the God-man, Jesus.

Jesus came as a Jewish man to reach the Jews. When it was time to reach the Romans, Peter was sent to a cultural gatekeeper, Cornelius. Did you ever wonder why God added that extra step in Acts 10? *Go send people to go find Peter and then have them send Peter back with them to finally get to Cornelius's house way up in Roman Caesarea.* Why not just send Cornelius himself to go learn from Peter? Because God values culture.

God consistently uses people as cultural bridges. Jesus called them persons of peace (Luke 10:6). God wanted Peter to struggle with entering a Roman home, something he had never done in his entire life due to laws of defilement and uncleanliness. God wanted the message to come to the gentiles on gentile turf. Peter needed to enter a Roman home in a Roman town named after a Roman emperor filled with Roman smells and Roman customs. Can you imagine what the church in Caesarea would have looked like if Peter had tried to incorporate all of his Jewish cultural assumptions regarding temple, priest and sacrifice?

This is why the church grows not through building expansion, but through DNA transfer. Physical temples are cumbersome. The Jerusalem temple took masons and woodworkers and goldsmiths to build it and an entire tribe of Levites to administrate it. It took enormous time, energy and resources.

Fourth place church expansion is the same. When we plant churches, first we need the team. Then we need the funds. Then we need the land. Then the building, the senior pastor, the administrative help, the worship leader, the children's director, the new sound system, the discipleship program, the evangelism person, and the list goes on and on. As the church grows, the list grows.

The way we develop churches is not only time-consuming and costly, but it is also culturally bound. With every decision regarding personnel, decor, worship style and preaching method comes a cultural decision. One style includes one or more cultures but excludes others. Not only does this isolate the church culturally, it also makes us continually obsolete. *Fourth place* church is in a perpetual fight between generations. This typically has much more to do with cultural preferences than theology or polity. What was brand new in the 1980s is now archaic. What was a timeless song is now overplayed or too loud. What used to be a fun basement for potlucks now has that funky church smell!

Not so with Jesus. A person as the temple is simple. Cost effective. Agile. Mobile. If you want to cross cultures, you don't need to hire a hip new worship pastor; just make a new friend. If you want to stay culturally relevant, you don't need a facility remodel; you just need some new pants.

With each DNA transfer the entire temple is at once moved into a new human being. They are now the temple as well. They now have Jesus himself dwelling in them through the Holy Spirit.

This is why the central strategy of an integrated church is *discipleship*. This is the process that brings about the DNA transfer in a person, helps that person be restored in the three spheres of their relationship with God, with others, and with their world, and eventually results in them reproducing the DNA in still more people.

Disciples, therefore, are the basic building blocks of the church. They are the living stones being built into a spiritual house (1 Pet. 2:5). They are the body made up of many members (Rom. 12:4). They are the temple of the Holy Spirit (1 Cor. 3:16). A disciple alone is not a church, but get some together and there you have church.

We practice communion as a reminder of WHO we are—a spiritual family related through Jesus' DNA. We practice baptism because it is a perfect picture of our entrance into a new family. When God wanted to get the temple into the farthest reaches of the earth, he didn't send a WHAT, he sent a WHO. He sent Jesus. Now he sends us.

The answer to our final question ("WHAT is the design for what we are trying to build?") is also not a WHAT but a WHO. God's design to accomplish his WHY is the church. The church is not an event in a building, the church is a spiritual family on mission together.

We have now come full circle. We know our WHY, we know our HOW, and we know we don't need a WHAT, but a WHO. Put them all together and here is a summary of the form and function of the church:

FUNCTION: The church is a spiritual family that exists to demonstrate integration with God, each other and our world.

Our function is why we exist, our purpose. What forms will help us accomplish our purpose?

FORM: Integrated place, people and practices.

The design we need is fundamentally different from the Christendom model. Constantine's foundation must be uprooted. Church is not a WHAT, but a WHO, and it is time for a new design.

Why Did It Work Before?

Some of you may be wondering what makes these concepts relevant for today. "Why is this just coming up now? Haven't our churches done a pretty good job discipling people in the past? And weren't they based around the paradigm of temple forms? Why do we suddenly need to change our design?"

The main reason is the major cultural shift in the West in the past century. Prior to the 1900s, much of the West still had a dominant cultural Christian identity. The church remained at the center of culture. Christendom was still working for many people because temple forms work well to promote and maintain a dominant culture.

Israel's temple was not separate from Israel; it was the very heart of Israel. The temple worked to promote and maintain Israel's national identity and ethos. This is the reason temple forms are still "working" (being attended) in some parts of Western culture. Much of the Bible Belt and small-town America has the building at the heart of their still-dominant Christian identity. There may be multiple denominational centers (one on each corner), but the culture still calls itself Christian.

But Christendom was built upon foundations that are quickly eroding. The Enlightenment, Industrial Revolution, and especially modern science and technology have undermined the dominant place of the church in culture.

The pastor's study used to be the locus of all good answers. Not so anymore. The lines demarcating spiritual and human have blurred. A century of psychology led by Freud and Jung show us that not all personality issues are spiritual in nature. Sometimes we need counseling or therapy rather than demon deliverance. Modern medicine shows us that not all healing comes from prayer. Of course we all need prayer, but sometimes we also need a vaccine. There is a blurring of East and West, spiritual and human. People are turning not only to pastors, but to fitness instructors, dietary experts, and the collective wisdom and experiences of the online community.

The idea that we need a holy man to dispense truth from a stage used to make sense culturally. Not anymore. We have instant access to a world of experts and podcasts. We don't need the pastor to show us pictures of faraway Israel when we have Google. Not only can we get any information we want, but we can also engage in the dialogue, express our own opinion and share it with a globally interconnected network.

Thankfully, these cultural changes are not a problem for Jesus, just Christendom. Jesus' life and teaching were holistic, not segregated in some sacred building. What is being dismantled is not Jesus, but the idea that religion can be kept to its own separate sphere of culture. The grand Christendom ideology has failed and what is left of the foundations are quickly crumbling. Alan Hirsch, in *The Forgotten Ways*, writes:

> People now identify themselves less by grand ideologies, national identities, political allegiances, and by much less grand stories: those of interest groups, new religious movements (New Age), sexual identity (gays, lesbians, transsexuals, etc.), sports activities, competing ideologies (neo-Marxist, neo-fascist, eco-rats, etc.), class, conspicuous consumption (metrosexuals, urban grunge, etc.), work types (computer geeks, hackers, designers, etc.), and so forth... Each of them takes their subcultural identity with utmost seriousness, and hence any missional response to them must as well.[63]

Cowboy Church
by Dudley Callison

My family roots extend back to small town, East Texas cowboy culture. I remember attending church on visits there. The farmers and ranchers dutifully washed and put on their "Sunday best" clothes. They also looked very uncomfortable. In order to attend church, they had to step outside of everything that felt normal to them. Their church day looked nothing like their every day. I was thrilled the first time I attended Cowboy Church. It gathered in a

---

[63] Hirsch, *Forgotten Ways*, 61.

local roping arena—the same place these churchgoers gathered on Friday night for the weekly roping. Some rode up on horseback. All of them wore jeans, boots and cowboy hats. The arena smelled just the same as always. The dirt broke beneath their boots. The band played songs they could relate to, including instruments that made them feel at home. Rather than asking them to step out of culture to be religious, Cowboy Church brought spirituality into their culture. I saw genuine followers of Christ enjoying Jesus in the place where they live, work and play.

In other words, Christendom has fractured. We have no cultural consensus, no grand unified ideology, no common philosophy. We are a culture of subcultures. Our fundamental struggle is that we are still using media designed around cultural consensus in a culture that has no cultural consensus.

Why are we doing this? Because it's all we know. When a hammer is your only tool in the tool bag, everything ends up looking like a nail. Leaders are trying to use *fourth places* (our hammer) to address these cultural challenges, and they are struggling. We are trying blended services across generations and ethnicity, and the cultural complexity is such that if your service meets the needs of two subcultures, you have still alienated fifty others. It isn't working.

The tools of the past cultural reality cannot solve the challenges of today. It is time to let go of our well-worn hammers and try out some new tools. We need a medium that is able to integrate with each subculture rather than asking them to meld with us. We need a medium that is able to engage the complexity of our humanity rather than imagining all answers are purely spiritual. We need a new design. Thankfully, our architect, Jesus, shows us the way toward a perfect design for every age.

Toward a Better Design

It is time to move toward forms of integration. We need to take practical steps to integrate our three forms of **place**, **people** and **practices** along the continuum from separation to integration. All of us are somewhere between separation and integration; it's not black and white.

In the past few chapters you have had the opportunity to figure out where you are currently on the chart regarding all three forms. The road forward will look different for all of us depending on our starting place and our capacity for change. What I am proposing is not one design that will fit every culture. Rather, I'm proposing a way of understanding church on a continuum of forms from separation to integration that can help any church, new or old, plot a course for better meeting their function.

We are going to get very practical in the coming chapters, but hopefully not limit you based on another person's experience or context. Just because there is no "right" way to do church does not mean all ways are equal. As we have seen, some structures promote separation by their very nature. Others promote integration. Some churches are promoting integration of **place** while promoting separation of **people**. All of us can grow more integrated across all three forms.

If you are a church planter or ready to experiment with new forms, the following chapters will give you all kinds of ideas for ways of living as an integrated church. If you have an existing church building and are wondering how you would ever move beyond forms of separation, change might need to be incremental and slower-paced.

Regardless, change is still possible. Wherever you are on the continuum, my hope is that you are inspired to take action.

Did Jesus Do This?

Change can be difficult. Some of you may have started reading and are now wondering if the cost of moving forward is worth it. I want to encourage you to embrace the journey ahead, not because I said it was a good idea, or showed how bad the alternative is, but because this is how our Lord Jesus lived.

In every way, Jesus showed us the way of an integrated church. Jesus is the living picture of the integration of all things. He showed an intimate and obedient relationship with his Father, a community where prostitutes and tax collectors are equal with religious leaders, and that mercy is better than sacrifice.

In Chapter 3, I talked about Jesus' encounter with the woman at the well as a paradigm shift in worship. Worship would no longer be about bringing people to the right temple, but about a mobile temple—people full of the Spirit of God. However, this story does not only show us a new paradigm of worship, but also a new wineskin of church and mission.

Our unnamed woman at the well asked Jesus the simple question, "Where is the right place to worship—Jerusalem or Samaria?" At the heart of her question is an underlying cultural question, "Who is God for? Jews or Samaritans? Which one needs to give up their cultural identity and submit to another way of being?"

My heart breaks even as I write this for the number of people throughout the world who have thought they need to become like a Western Christian in order to worship God. But not Jesus. His answer to this woman is an overwhelming, "No!" He says, *a time is coming when worship will integrate with your culture in a way that restores you to your creator without your people having to become like the Jews.* Jesus does not separate the people of Sychar into a new culture; he demonstrates to them how the kingdom can integrate with Samaria.

Look at how Jesus models integration in the three forms of **place**, **people** and **practices**:

Place: Jesus meets them on their turf, in their town, at their *third place*—the well. The well was integral to their cultural life. This is where people had to come for water. This is where community interaction took place. Of course Jesus went there. That was his norm. He lived and moved and walked where people lived. Jesus modeled the integration of **place**.

People: Jesus goes straight to the bottom. He doesn't seek out the mayor or create a billboard advertisement. He goes to someone on the fringes, someone barely hanging on. He asks her for a drink. Jews don't do that. Men don't do that. But that was his norm. Everywhere Jesus went he raised up valleys, brought down mountains and made a level road. Jesus lived out the integration of **people**.

Practices: Jesus shows mercy and compassion toward an outcast woman. He confronts systems of injustice. When he is invited into the lives of the people of the town, he goes. He doesn't invite them to the synagogue next door. He shares their normal life with them for two days. He eats their food and joins their families. Jesus lives out the integration of **practices**.

This is how Jesus lived. This is what Jesus modeled for his apostles who would plant the first churches. Shouldn't we, then, follow his example in the way we build our churches?

It is time to build. We now know our function and we understand the forms that will align our medium with our message. In the next chapters we will look at what it means to build churches using integrated forms now familiar to you: **place**, **people** and **practices**.

9

Church in Exile

My family and I moved in 2010 to Denver, Colorado, so I could go to Denver Seminary. Our first October in our new neighborhood a bunch of the other dads invited me to take part in their Halloween tradition. They would take the kids out trick-or-treating while pulling a wagon full of beer for the men. The moms would stay back home and drink wine. Welcome to Colorado! While out on the streets, I started up a conversation with one of the men as he smoked on his pipe. We quickly realized we were both followers of Jesus. He found out I was attending Denver Seminary, and I learned that he was the President of a church-planting organization called Communitas International.

Yes, I met Dudley while trick-or-treating. Somehow, God in his wisdom planted us right in the middle of his family's mission to love their neighborhood. You can imagine our shock in happening upon someone with such a similar heart, having just moved out of our Tacoma neighborhood where we had invested years of our lives in shared mission with some of our best friends.

Dudley has an incredible heart for his neighbors. People trust him. They randomly show up on his porch for a beer and a conversation about life. He is a great listener—more interested in the right question than the right answer. One of my favorite memories of Dudley was watching him baptize a married couple from the neighborhood at a nearby lake. Half the people who lived on the street, believers and not, were in attendance.

Dudley ended up mentoring me through my seminary process. Along the way we started a spiritual discussion group with several other neighbor families, some professing Christians, others not sure how to label themselves. In our first few gatherings we shared with each other the story of our own spiritual journey. One of the women in the group I had met through coaching her daughter's soccer team. Our daughters were close friends. When she shared her story there wasn't a dry eye in the room. She detailed experience after experience of spiritual abuse and betrayal brought about by leaders in their church. It was no wonder she wanted nothing to do with organized religion.

Over time, people slowly began to trust each other and feel a sense of safe community. People who formerly expressed anger at church started referring to our group as "neighbor church." One night, Dudley had just come home from a trip to Europe and was explaining what the Communitas churches were doing about the recent Syrian refugee crisis. I remember Dudley feeling such a burden for the refugees, what he described as the collateral damage of other people's bombs and decisions. Dudley felt frustrated that he could do so little from so far away in Denver. After he shared, the same woman who had been so hurt by the church said, "I know you are concerned for the refugees, but I just want to thank you for being here with us. We feel like spiritual refugees. We are the collateral damage of the church's abuse, and you are here helping us pick up the pieces."

I open with this story to simply say that this idea of church in culture is real. This is not just good theory for the classroom or the ivory tower of academia. This impacts real lives. God made the temple into flesh and it matters for you and it matters for your neighbors. Out of love, God tore his presence from behind the curtain and moved into the neighborhood.

Some people will still show up at our church buildings on Sunday morning, but most won't. Most don't even have church on their radar. Most aren't thinking about which church to attend or which one has the best preacher. Most people don't even care. Many that do care are angry with church. All of that stuff we do during the week to prepare for great services has no impact on their lives. The Beatles song, *Eleanor Rigby*, captures reality pretty well. "Father MacKenzie, writing a sermon that no one will hear. No one comes near."

People simply aren't coming to our buildings. Those who actually *do* show up aren't seeing Jesus. They are seeing worship bands and hearing sermons. As Dudley says, "My unchurched neighbors aren't waiting for churches to adjust their preaching style or music in order to show up. They're waiting for people to actually live and act like Jesus."

How can people see Jesus if the church, his body, will not come to them? We need to talk about **place** if we are to be a living demonstration of God's reconciliation in the real world, a visible demonstration of the love of God. The basic principle of an integrated church regarding **place** is this: **we do church from within culture, not separate from it.**

Out of the Fourth Place

We must leave the *fourth place*, because that's what God did in Christ. He left behind the days of religion as **a holy place where holy people do holy things** and he sent his Son right into the mess and beauty of his broken creation. From here to here:

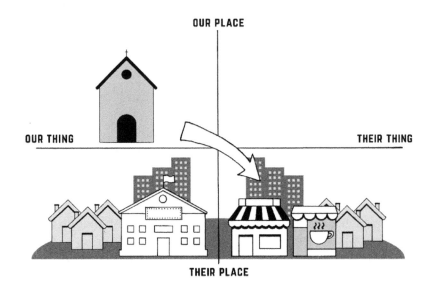

Jesus left OUR PLACE. He didn't invite people to a sacred building; he was the building. He didn't bring them before a holy priest; he was the priest. He didn't create a liturgy or culture of formal worship practices; he was the sacrifice.

As followers of Jesus, if we are to match our medium with our message, we are to do the same. So where do we start?

Into the First, Second and Third Place

I want to propose a way to think about and practice **place** starting from Oldenburg's model of *first, second* and *third places*—the places we live, work and play. As we have seen, our current concept of church has occupied a *fourth place* (formal public life). So how do we come out of the *fourth place*? We come out of our religious buildings, and integrate our churches, our spiritual families, into the normal fabric of our surrounding culture.

If you are NOT starting from an existing building-based context, this will mean starting church from the context of relationships in *first, second* and *third* places. If you ARE starting with a building, this will mean both converting your building, or parts of it, into *first, second* or *third places,* as well as creating a culture in your church that sees ministry outside the building as equally, if not more valid than ministry inside the building. This chapter will give you ideas for what both approaches can look like.

Wherever you are starting from, a key biblical image and theological foundation that will help us navigate how to do church within culture is the Old Testament story of the exile. A woman in our Neighbor Church claimed to be a spiritual refugee. Refugees and exiles have a lot in common; neither feel at home in their world. As we explore the exile we will see how to engage our world without losing our identity as Christ followers. We will see that it is possible to be BOTH fully identified with Christ AND fully integrated with our world.

Exiles in Tension

Now some of you may be wondering how the church can keep its identity and passion alive if we let go of our buildings. We know that our buildings have led to much of our dysfunction, but they also keep us grounded. When someone attends a service and says with a sigh of relief, "I have finally found my church home," we see that our buildings and events give us a sense of security and identity. They give us a sense of home.

As we think about leaving the *fourth place* and integrating with our culture, a couple of questions are sure to come up: Where do we find our identity if not in our buildings? How do we affirm and engage our culture without giving up what it means to follow Christ? How do we integrate with our world without losing the gospel?

These are great questions, and they speak of the tension believers experience in trying to be relevant to the world and yet retaining our own unique Christian identity. Thankfully the Bible is not silent about answering these questions. During their period of exile, God's chosen people were removed from their homeland and brought into captivity in Babylon. Jews whose very lifestyle and culture centered around the temple system were now forced to live in a country they despised. Struggling to know how to live, the exiles received instructions from God through the prophet Jeremiah:

> This is what the LORD Almighty, the God of Israel, says to all those I carried into exile from Jerusalem to Babylon: "Build houses and settle down; plant gardens and eat what they produce. Marry and have sons and daughters; find wives for your sons and give your daughters in marriage, so that they too may have sons and daughters. Increase in number there; do not decrease. Also, seek the peace and prosperity of the city to which I have carried you into exile. Pray to the LORD for it, because if it prospers, you too will prosper."
>
> Jeremiah 29:4-7

While every fiber of their being longed to be back in their own homeland, centering their lives around the temple, God told them to seek the prosperity of Babylon. *Integrate with the people you despise. Touch the people who make you unclean. Pray for the city that conquered you and stole everything you hold dear.*

Do you feel the tension? How could God's chosen people defile themselves by integrating with their enemy, Babylon? How can the holy mix with the unholy? Jeremiah's instructions are a paradox—two seemingly impossible truths held together at once. It is so much easier to remove the tension. Either fight against culture OR succumb to culture. The exile gives us another option. The exile tells us it is a *both/and*, not an *either/or*. We are to maintain our unique identity that is counter-cultural AND we are to love and serve our Babylon. How do we do this? It starts with the example of Jesus, the model exile.

Jesus the Exile

Jesus lived this tension perfectly. In fact, the tension was sewn into his very being. Jesus is fully God AND fully human. Fully of the Spirit AND fully flesh and blood. Fully separate from culture in his identity, purity and holiness, AND fully a Jewish male who had to get up and go to work like the rest of us.

The incarnation is a picture of exile—God himself without his home. If the church's purpose is to be a living picture of reconciliation with God, with each other and with the world, the way to accomplish this is to pattern our churches after Jesus, the exile.

You see, temples, priests and rituals are the natural way for Christians to resolve the tension. We don't use these words, of course. We call them facilities, staff and programs. After all, what does every exile long for? Home. It is natural for Christians to want our own religious complexes (**place**). It feels safe. It gives us a secure identity. And after we get our promised land, just like Israel, we ask for a king (**people**). We want a successful senior pastor. We want a figurehead to lead our cause. Finally, we want our own worship culture (**practices**). We want comfortable sounds, lyrics and smells that will protect our families from the influences of the world. Our temple forms, our *fourth places*, resolve the cultural tension.

Jesus, on the other hand, stands in opposition to these easily resolved tensions. Jesus' life represents a life in exile. He left his home in heaven and chose a life with no place to lay his head. He refused to become king by force. Rather than demanding temple excellence, he healed the blind and the lame. He sought the peace of his beloved Jerusalem. What was true of Jesus must be true of the church. We are to leave behind OUR PLACE and make our home in our culture.

The writers of The New Testament identified the church as a community in exile. Peter opens his first letter stating, "Peter, an apostle of Jesus Christ, to God's elect, exiles scattered throughout the provinces of Pontus, Galatia, Cappadocia, Asia and Bithynia…" (1 Peter 1:1). James opens his letter, "James, a servant of God and of the Lord Jesus Christ, to the twelve tribes scattered among the nations" (James 1:1). He uses the image of the twelve tribes scattered to identify them as the people of exile.

The writer of Hebrews encourages Christians to stay strong by exemplifying the heroes of faith. He writes,

> All these people were still living by faith when they died. They did not receive the things promised; they only saw them and welcomed them from a distance, admitting that they were foreigners and strangers on earth. People who say such things show that they are looking for a country of their own. If they had been thinking of the country they had left, they would have had opportunity to return. Instead, they were longing for a better country—a heavenly one. Therefore God is not ashamed to be called their God, for he has prepared a city for them.
>
> Hebrews 11:13-16

Jesus and the early church thought of themselves as strangers in a country not their own. So must we. And yet, there is a balance. Though we are people of exile, we are also people of the promise. Though we live in human bodies, even now we have the downpayment of our future inheritance, the promised Holy Spirit. There is a *now* and *not-yet* nature of the kingdom in which we live. We are strangers within our own culture and yet, Paul writes the following in Ephesians 2:19-22:

Consequently, you are no longer foreigners and strangers, but fellow citizens with God's people and also members of his household, built on the foundation of the apostles and prophets, with Christ Jesus himself as the chief cornerstone. In him the whole building is joined together and rises to become a holy temple in the Lord. And in him you too are being built together to become a dwelling in which God lives by his Spirit.

This is not a contradiction; it is a tension. We are strangers in the physical world, yet we are being built into a temple in the spiritual realm. We have no home, yet we are at home in Christ. We are a living temple, only you can't see it with the physical eye. Not yet. Not while we are still in exile in the world. The ages have overlapped. We are at once deeply satisfied in Christ and yet we long for the reconciliation of all things, the true return to our promised land.

How then do we live in this tension?

We come out of the *fourth place*. We refuse to build a physical temple. We refuse to build our perfect home.

Instead, we focus on building a spiritual temple, a network of people, right in the midst of culture.

A New Starting Place

Here is how we typically practice church. We start with OUR THING in OUR PLACE and we work outward.

Even our terms like "outreach" reveal our fundamental orientation which puts our building at the safe center of religious life.

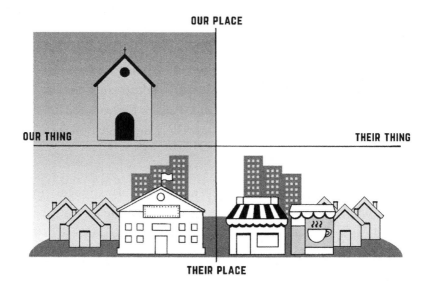

Most of what we call church happens in the building. This includes worship services, staff office hours, counseling, Bible studies, women's ministry, discipleship classes and youth group. Some churches also move "out" into the OUR THING, THEIR PLACE quadrant. This is our small groups program in the home. But regardless of what else is added, the core of the church and the financial engine are attached to the building.

Contrasted with this building-centric approach is an **integrated church**. An integrated church spends most of its time, energy and resources in the THEIR THING, THEIR PLACE quadrant. Its gatherings take place in the OUR THING, THEIR PLACE quadrant. In either case, gathered or scattered, the life of the church happens in and among culture.

In other words, an integrated church starts from the exact opposite side of the four quadrants.

It looks like this:

An integrated church is able to do this because it is built on a fundamentally different foundation, a WHO, not a WHAT. Church, as we have discussed at length, is not primarily an event in a building. Church is people. Church is a community, a spiritual family. If we believe this, then church must start not as an event, but as a relationship. We find our home not in our sacred space, but in our sacred family, our community.

Exiles in Scotland

Communitas International starts churches in culture. They don't start by trying to draw people to cool new events; they start by living among the people. Their first step of church planting is to simply embed within the culture for a period of time.

One Communitas church planter couple is currently embedded in Leith, Scotland, a poorer city on the outskirts of Edinburgh. These church planters hang around the apartment complex commons. They show up at local restaurants. They spend time in the dirt and conversation of the community garden. As they do this, they meet people, they listen, and they begin to understand the needs of Leith.

Communitas calls this listening process, *exegeting the culture*. They are discerning how the gospel and the culture need to intersect. They don't assume they are the first ones to bring God into that place. Instead they are looking for what God is already up to. They do not assume what form the church gathering will take, they simply start from the posture of listeners, servants and friends.

Having embedded for some time, this young couple is currently working to start communities of faith in several apartments in their area, *first places*. Why apartments? Because they listened. This is where God provided their initial relationships. Gathering in apartments makes sense for that community.

They started in THEIR THING, THEIR PLACE and they are slowly moving to include OUR THING, THEIR PLACE as the community matures.

Like this:

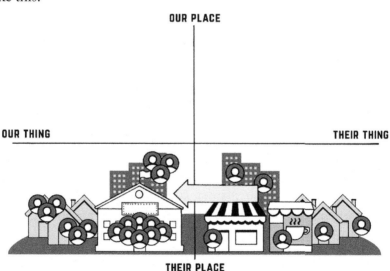

What started as seemingly random relationships in the *first place*, the apartment complex, and the *third place*, the community garden, are now turning into communities of faith.

Redemption of Place

Coming out of the fourth place is not a rejection of holy places but instead the affirmation that God has made possible the redemption of ALL places. The torn veil of the temple, as much as it had to do with allowing humans into God's presence, was just as much about God leaving the building. It represented a movement back to *the everywhere worship of Eden.*

"Coming out of the fourth place is not a rejection of holy places but instead the affirmation that God has made possible the redemption of ALL places."

If Eden hadn't fallen, THEIR THING, THEIR PLACE is the only quadrant that would have ever existed. Remember, there were no religious buildings in Eden—no OUR PLACE. There will be no religious buildings in the new heaven and the new earth. THEIR PLACE is where people are born, get married, raise kids and go to a baseball game. It is the place of our careers, dreams, productivity, art, politics, meals, families and commerce.

THEIR PLACE is the place of discipleship. Why? Because this is where we learn how to live like Jesus in the world. This is where we learn to be truly human. To put us in the building is to remove discipleship from its natural context. It's like trying to teach someone how to fish by taking them to a seafood restaurant. It doesn't work! We learn to be a follower of Jesus as we follow him directly into the core of our humanity.

Exiles in Santa Barbara

A group of Communitas church planters embedded themselves in Santa Barbara, California. They watched. They observed. They listened. They served. What they witnessed were two groups of people with vast needs. The first they noticed were the homeless—thousands of them. Homeless people would congregate in Pershing Park, a *third place*, so that's where they started to build friendships. They fed the people in the park, and as they did, a movement began and more people joined in the efforts.

While the needs of the homeless were obvious, the needs of the more affluent Christian community were less visible at first. Eventually it became clear these more affluent believers were suffering from a deep consumerism and a real lack of faith. The church planters decided to do something about both needs. They gathered weekly in the park for a feeding program where both the homeless and the affluent learn from one another what it means to follow Christ. Along the way, they formed a group of committed friends that became known as the Uffitzi Missional Order—a new monastic community. Together they have committed themselves to a rule of life that helps them maintain their unique identity as followers of Christ and yet fully engage the needs of their city.

Are They a Church?

Some reading this may be wondering where they gather and how often, whether they take communion and how big they are. If those are your first questions, you are still thinking of church as primarily an event in a building. You are thinking about a WHAT, not a WHO. Do they take communion? Yes, every week in the park with one hundred homeless people. Do they worship? Yes, they regularly lay down their lives sacrificially for trafficked women on the streets.

This is a small group of Christ-followers making a big difference as they seek the peace of Santa Barbara. They are a spiritual family on mission together. They are demonstrating reconciliation with God, with each other and with their world. This is a church. This small new monastic community will not likely be featured in *Relevant Magazine*. They do not care about stage design or lighting concepts. Still, they are the church, a beautiful expression of Christ's body on earth.

Start AND Stay in Culture

When we start in THEIR PLACE, we don't need to invite them to our buildings. We join them where they already live. We grab a coffee. We have a dinner. Our kids play together. We go to a game. Eventually we share our spiritual stories. We listen. We offer our own story. We serve them when they have a need. We allow them to serve us when we have a need. We become family. The normalness of life together defines our relationship.

When church attendance starts as an event in *OUR PLACE*, we have to work really hard to keep people happy and make them stick. When church starts as a relationship, you already have the glue. You start with a normal relationship. You don't have to try to sell people or train greeters. You don't need flashy marketing materials. Connection is natural, not artificial. Eventually, normal life together might lead to gathered life as a community of faith.

This movement simply indicates that we are gathering on purpose because we are Christians. That's what happened in our Neighbor Church in Denver. We were already sharing our spiritual journeys. Giving it a name and a regular meeting time simply made it official. Hugh Halter, in his book, *Tangible Kingdom*, describes a group of people, neither insiders nor outsiders, whom he calls *sojourners*.[64] These

---

[64] Halter and Smay, *The Tangible Kingdom*, 116.

are the people who are somewhere along the faith journey. They are checking out your community, but they are not yet committed to Jesus. The blurring of the bottom two quadrants makes this group possible. Since you spend most of your time in THEIR PLACE, they are part of your life and relational sphere. Since you gather in THEIR PLACE, they feel your community is accessible to them when they are ready to join. They don't have to make the leap from THEIR PLACE to OUR PLACE, from their culture to our religious culture. That is a chasm many are simply not willing to cross, nor should they have to.

An integrated church does not just *start* within culture, but intentionally *stays* within culture. Many school-based church planters long for the day they ditch the set-up trailer and have a church building of their own, but that is not the goal of an integrated church. We think more like Young Life and other parachurch organizations. The goal of Young Life is not to start up a club in a school in order to eventually raise enough money from families to one day leave the school and buy their own building. That would be ridiculous. Why? Because it violates the very purpose of Young Life—to love kids where they are. Church is a WHO, not a WHAT, and they have put themselves in the right position to reach people for Christ.

Exiles in France

Two Communitas church planters moved to France to plant a church. They landed in a town that had recently been inundated with refugee families. As they began to embed within the community it became quickly apparent that every civic entity, from the schools to the courts, was in a conundrum as to how to respond to the refugee crisis. They listened. They exegeted culture. Eventually, they found an opportunity to get certified as childcare workers and went to work helping mostly Muslim children integrate into the school system. They run an after-school program for tutoring, language development and character formation. They take kids to adventure camps where they learn relevant life skills.

In Muslim culture, to bless one's kids is to bless the entire family. They have now developed deep relationships with many Muslim families and were even invited by a Tunisian elder to accompany a recently deceased community member's body back to Tunisia and offer a prayer of blessing at their Muslim memorial service. Community is forming and the church is being birthed even among a primarily Muslim immigrant culture. Embedding within culture opens doors to connecting with people who will never enter our buildings.

Exiles in St. Paul

In Communitas Twin Cities, Diana McCarten is catalyzing a community of people deeply committed to each other and to serving local needs. They run a winter boot drive in St. Paul, Minnesota, to collect and give away thousands of boots every year. They have monthly access to a food truck that feeds enormous numbers of local homeless. They don't use a building; they don't have a mortgage. Resources are free to bless the city. People participate in communion with God, community with each other and service for the world. This church is a living picture of the exile, this time not in Babylon, but in St. Paul.

What would it look like to seek the peace of your city? What if you took all the time, energy and money spent on maintaining a nice facility and put that toward your neighbors? Imagine what could happen!

The Power of a Network

Communitas is just one example of a network supporting people around the world who are trying to be church in the culture. There are many others. I am telling a lot of Communitas stories because I want you to experience church not as one individual building and its occupants, but as a relational network spread throughout the world. When we hear the stories of normal exiles scattered throughout a variety of cultures, we realize that we can be a part of it. Church planting is not a sport for lone rangers on their heroic journey. Church planting is the work of a mature network who prays for each other, supports one another and releases people with a variety of gifts and passions into every corner of the globe.

The Danger of the Ideal

Many people think about church planting with an end product already in mind—an ideal WHAT. "This is WHAT I'm called to do." For example, one might imagine they are called to go start a hipster-style worship service in a cool urban setting. This vision becomes a deeply held dream that all their efforts work to produce. Deitrich Bonhoeffer had a lot to say about this approach in his book, *Life Together*.

> Every human wish dream that is injected into the Christian community is a hindrance to genuine community and must be banished if genuine community is to survive. He who loves his dream of a community more that the Christian community itself becomes a destroyer of the latter, even though his personal intentions may be ever so honest and earnest and sacrificial.[65]

Bonhoeffer talks about the importance of starting with real people, a WHO. He encouraged people to learn to see Christ in each other—in real, broken, irritating people. Instead, today, we so often start with an *ideal*, a WHAT, and then attempt to force everyone into that vision. Bonhoeffer says this method of church will always be surrounded by human wisdom and selfish ambition. In my own experience, I have seen

---

[65] Deitrich Bonhoeffer, *Life Together* (San Francisco, CA: Harper & Row Publishers, 1954), 27.

many wonderful people burned and rejected by church leaders because they didn't quite fit the pastor's vision of the *ideal*.

In these cases, the problem is an improper starting point. They started with an *ideal fourth place*, their dream event in their dream space. They started with WHAT they were trying to create and then manipulated those around them to help create it. That is not how an integrated church works. An integrated church starts with WHO. We embed within a place. We meet real people. We develop real relationships. We allow church to form naturally out of the actual people who are a part of the community. It's messy because people are messy. There is nothing *ideal* about it. That's the beauty of church. That's the gospel. God takes broken people and calls us beautiful.

Church is a WHO, not a WHAT. So then, if the most important question is WHO, what does that mean about **place**? It means that church can form anywhere there are people. While it may sound obvious, our obsession with the *ideal* often limits the wonderful possibilities of places where we can find people.

Maybe you have a vision in your head of a coffee shop church. Maybe it's a brewery church. Maybe it's a concert venue church. Great, maybe God will use one of those expressions of church in the *third place*, but don't start with the event in mind, start with the people in mind. Listen to them. Who are they? What are their dreams? Where do they want to gather? Using the model of *first*, *second* and *third places* may open up some ideas you have never considered.

First Place Church Forms

The most obvious type of *first place* church is the house church. Networks of house churches are a beautiful way to integrate with the *first place*. Beyond the primary residence, we need to reach apartment complexes. Many of them have common spaces that could be used for a gathering. Apartment Life is a ministry with a great model to love and reach people in multifamily units.[66] Remember, there's more to the neighborhood than just homes. Dudley and I saw about forty neighbors come out to a Christmas party we threw at our local neighborhood swim club. Some of these same people were eventually a part of the Neighbor Church.

Second Place Church Forms

What about work? What types of gathering spaces does your work provide? Many offices have conference rooms, cafeterias or exercise facilities that are great places to gather. When I worked at Russell Investments, a group of about ten of us met weekly before work to discuss a book and pray for each other.

Statistics show that by the year 2020, 40 percent of the workforce will operate outside of the traditional office space.[67] To meet the need for community among a largely independent workforce, coworking businesses are popping up all over the world. Communitas actually owns and operates one called The Guild in Englewood, Colorado. What if you joined a coworking space and got groups together for lunch or to view a TED talk on a popular business topic? What a perfect place to connect with people, hear their business dreams and share life.

The *second place* for adults is work, but for kids and many others it is school or college. What if you started building relationships by joining your local PTA? What if you helped tutor kids after school? Young Life and Youth for Christ have done a great job emphasizing contact work at the schools. They hang out at football games and risk humiliation in

---

[66] For more information, visit www.apartmentlife.org.
[67] Richard Henderson, "Employment Outlook: 2010-2020," *Bureau of Labor Review* (January 2012), https://www.bls.gov/opub/mlr/2012/01/art4full.pdf.

middle school cafeterias for the sake of loving kids. What if you simply joined what they are already doing?

One of the big questions about integrated churches is what to do with our youth. What if, instead of hiring an expensive youth pastor, you partner with Young Life? A volunteer from your community could lead a Young Life small group (Campaigners) and take advantage of the amazing camps, service opportunities, discipleship and training Young Life has to offer.

There is no need to reinvent the wheel for our teenagers. If adults are learning to get out of the *fourth place* and into the world, why shouldn't our kids? That's how we all grow to live more like Jesus.

Third Place Church Forms

The church has done a pretty good job thinking creatively about *third places*. We have churches meeting in concert venues, theaters, pubs and coffee shops. However, too often we have only viewed these spaces as temporary locations until we can afford our own place. What if we were okay staying smaller and remaining where people gather? What if we were okay living as exiles permanently?

Many other opportunities for *third place* churches exist as well. If we are in the suburbs, we may want to consider forming church starting from the soccer field. How would we structure church if we thought of kids' activities as a blessing rather than a distraction? There are so many places people hang out that aren't even on the radar of many church planters—city councils, fitness centers, youth clubs, AA, the running community, the cycling community and many others. Some of these may seem less cool, but that's the point. We start where people actually are.

Where are the people in your world? Are you doing church with them or are you hiding in a church building trying to keep the machine running? What would it look like to leave the *fourth place* behind and seek the peace of your city together with a group of friends?

Hope for the Established Church

Some of you are saying at this point, "Great, that sounds fun to hang out with people in the midst of culture, but we have a building with a mortgage. We have people who are accustomed to a particular way of doing church and they expect me to be at my church office desk morning, noon and night."

Here is where good theory faces practical reality. Jesus said that new wine will often burst old wineskins. Maybe you are afraid that making huge changes will cause your congregation to implode. You may be right. This is where you have to be wise and prayerful in your application of this book. If you have a building and still want to make incremental change toward integration of **place**, the following chart can help you understand three potential directions for change.

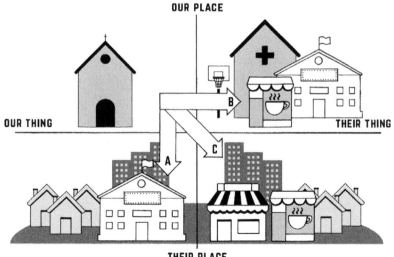

A. OUR THING, THEIR PLACE

If you are in a church that focuses almost entirely in OUR PLACE, the most obvious first step is to balance it out with OUR THING, THEIR PLACE. Books like *Simple Church*[68], *Sticky Church*[69] and *Discipleshift*[70] offer great first steps for building out solid small groups programs that get people out of the building and into the *first place*, the home.

If you are already doing small groups, but still struggling with discipleship, there are many factors that play into this. Books like *Building a Discipling Culture* (3DM)[71] and ministries like Faith Walking[72] can help churches move from surface-level-commuter small groups to more intentional discipleship.

B. THEIR THING, OUR PLACE

Another largely untapped opportunity for the established church might lie right in front of your nose—the building itself. Many churches are turning what used to be a religion-only zone into a legitimate *first*, *second* or *third place* for the community. Perhaps this means starting a public coffee shop or leasing out some of your space to businesses. It could simply mean allowing AA, Girl Scouts or the PTA to use your space. Perhaps you could be an emergency shelter for the Red Cross. In allowing your neighborhood to utilize your building for their needs, homes, businesses and activities, you are blurring the lines between sacred and secular and reintegrating yourself into the fabric of your community.

---

[68] Rainer and Geiger, *Simple Church*.
[69] Larry Osborne, *Sticky Church* (Grand Rapids: Zondervan, 2008).
[70] Jim Putnam and Bobby Harrington with Robert E. Coleman, *Discipleshift* (Grand Rapids: Zondervan, 2013).
[71] Breen and Cockram, *Building a Discipling Culture*.
[72] For more information, visit www.faithwalking.us.

Repurposed
by Dudley Callison

In the mid-1800s, Westbourne Grove became a large, vibrant congregation on the West side of London. The building grew to an early prototype of what we would call a megachurch today. London grew and changed, and the congregation became more remote as people moved out to the suburbs. Eventually the membership shrank and the local neighborhood ignored the large, irrelevant facility on the corner. The membership became too small to maintain the facility.

An innovative pastor came along and asked the key question, "What would it take for this church to become relevant to our neighborhood again?" The first problem was financial capital. To solve this, the church sold the roof structure to an apartment developer who converted the space into luxury lofts. The proceeds were used to renovate the remaining space into a modern-day community center, complete with a large hall for weddings, dances and art exhibits. The other rooms were transformed for community classes, parties, language classes, children's clubs and many other uses.

Today, more than one thousand groups book space in the church each year, and thousands of local people move in and out of the facility. The church staff manage the bookings and offer Christ-centered hospitality to all who enter. Through this, believers have come to know many of the neighborhood residents, opening doors to bless and minister in the name of Jesus. And the neighborhood loves them in return.

Opening up your church building to the community is not only fiscally preferable, but far better for your mission. North Seattle Church has a prime piece of lakefront real estate in the middle of Seattle. The church used to be a fortress within the neighborhood, only used for church activities, but that has all changed. Now a choir organization and non-Christian preschool both lease space. The church opens the lakefront area for community BBQs and swimming each summer. They have converted an old classroom into The Bridge Coffee House. Eighty percent of the coffee shop revenue comes from the neighborhood. In other words, what was formerly a fortress has been accepted back into the community as a legitimate *second* and *third place*.

What about your building? Can it be embraced by the neighborhood? Some buildings can. Some can't. Some are designed with such an insiders-only mentality that they will never be an asset to the community. This is where you need wisdom. Will you end up pastoring a dying fortress, or are you ready to move on and integrate with your culture?

C. THEIR THING, THEIR PLACE

As a church we are so used to creating every idea from the center and asking everyone to join us. We plan it, and the congregation volunteers to help out. What if you flipped this? What if you created a space for people to dream on their own about their own neighbors, streets and civic issues? Instead of creating a tutoring program at your building, join an existing one at a school. Instead of building your own coffee shop and staffing it, drink someone else's coffee. Go to their event and join their parties. That is what Jesus did.

Beyond these three directions, changes to the *fourth place* itself are also possible. Take a walk with your staff or an architect through your facility and ask the question, "What are our forms saying? Is this a club for Christians or this is a safe place for everyone?" Make changes. Install some windows so people can see in. Instead of having a door that looks like a gothic castle entryway, put in a glass door. Open up your lobby. Put in comfortable seating. Take down the wallpaper and cross-stitch; instead, ask a local artist to display their work.

Incremental change is possible but prepare for opposition. Alan Roxburgh, in his book *Introducing the Missional Church*[73], offers a helpful model for moving a church through this difficult change process. Ultimately, you have to decide whether the benefits outweigh the costs.

Whether you are part of a new wineskin of integrated churches or part of the *fourth place* wineskin hoping for incremental change, the end goal is the same. **We are moving church toward integration of place**. We do church where people live. We do church like Jesus. Like exiles.

Onto Other Forms

Sounds pretty simple, right? Do church from within culture, not separate from it. Some of you may be thinking, "Yes, let's do it!" Others are thinking, "Embedding and listening sounds nice, but a church planter needs to become self-sustaining and bring in a strong tithe. Otherwise, it will never work financially."

You may be right. If integration with **place** were the only form that mattered, the financial model may be broken. It might not work. That is why we must also talk about integration in our other two forms: **people** and **practices**. One without the others is a set-up for failure or frustration. In fact, this is what many church planters are facing. Those who are running "church in a box" church plants know what this feels

---

[73] Alan J. Roxburgh and M. Scott Boren, *Introducing the Missional Church* (Grand Rapids: Baker Books, 2009).

like. They are attempting to integrate with cultural places—they meet in a school or a concert venue—so they store all of their worship stuff in a trailer instead of keeping it on stage. Their **place** is integrated, but not their **people** or their **practices**. They still set up everything for the standard leader on the stage and the typical worship set. Setting up for a *fourth place* service in a shared *third place* every weekend is a lot of work! I suspect many of you know what I mean.

There is hope. In the next chapter we will address the integration of **people**. What does it mean to be a kingdom of priests? What does church look like when we flatten the mountains and raise up the valleys, blurring the divide between clergy and laity? In order to do church in the *first*, *second* and *third* places of culture we will need to fundamentally rethink our approach to Christian leadership.

10

Church Is an All-Play

More than a decade ago, Communitas planted Upper Room Church in Glasgow, Scotland. Upper Room is a community of about forty-five Iranian immigrants. They gather in a large apartment around a community meal speaking in their native language, Farsi.

Everything about the Upper Room Church is what my friend Dudley calls an *all-play*. The whole night is full of active community participation. Anyone can take part in the meal preparation. The cooking begins in the early afternoon and culminates in an elaborate meal lasting well into the evening. Teaching is also an *all-play* since it is less about didactic sermonizing and more about the facilitation of dialogue. Then they sing. This time it is a literal *all-play* where anyone can bring an instrument and play along. Next they pray—not just the pastor, but the whole community. They hang out, enjoy some more food, and around 10 p.m. most of them head home.

Many people have come to faith in Christ through the Upper Room Church. The story heard over and over again goes something like this:

"I thought I knew what Christianity was from a distance, but I didn't consider following Jesus until I saw it lived out in the home." As more people came to faith, more of them started to participate in the community. As more participated, the Communitas church planters slowly handed over leadership to the Iranians.

And then something unexpected happened. One of the Communitas church planters was walking through the apartment complex and bumped into an Iranian he didn't recognize. They greeted each other and began a conversation in which the Iranian man mentioned that he was a part of the "Wednesday night Upper Room Church." The church planter was disoriented because they met on Fridays, not Wednesdays.

"No, you must be confused, we meet on Fridays. And why don't I recognize you? I'm there every week."

It turned out that one of the Iranian leaders who had been part of the Friday gathering started a Wednesday evening gathering for those who couldn't make Friday nights. On his own, he started up a church gathering—a meal, dialogue about Jesus, singing, prayer—and now more Iranian immigrants have come to Christ through this new expression on Wednesday nights. It was a new gathering, and the original church planters didn't even know about it!

This story raises some interesting questions. Some of you may be thinking, "Whoa! That sounds a little out of control. We don't want people just starting up churches whenever they want to. How do we even know what they are teaching?"

We'll get to that question later. For now, I want to focus on a different question—what was it about this Friday night *all-play* church that made an Iranian immigrant be able to say, "Yes, I could start up another gathering like that. Yes, I feel qualified"? And what makes so many of us in the West think we are *unqualified* to pastor a church?

When I was the small groups pastor at a church of seven thousand people, we went through a senior pastor transition. After a year of intense searching, interviews, and listening to literally hundreds of sermons, the search team still had no qualified leads.

How can a year of searching for a pastor yield no qualified candidates, yet an Iranian immigrant who had just come to Christ is able to launch a new church on his own?

Acts 4:13 says, "When they saw the courage of Peter and John and realized that they were unschooled, ordinary men, they were astonished and they took note that these men had been with Jesus." When did church leadership shift from unschooled, ordinary people who had been with Jesus to a professional class? When did church stop being an *all-play*?

In Chapter 6, we took a hard look at the role of leadership in the church and discovered that our basic pastoral job description didn't come from Jesus' method of feeding and growing sheep, but from a Roman emperor's desire to feed his own ego and grow his own kingdom.

If we are going to rebuild the temple, not out of bricks and mortar, but out of *living stones*, then we must rebuild our paradigm of Christian leadership. The basic principle regarding our **people** is this: **the church is a community of mutual participation and shared responsibility.** Church is an *all-play*.

But how do we do this?

How do we change from being a culture obsessed with big and talented celebrity leaders to a culture of mutual participation?

Again, the answer lies in our starting point.

The way to reintegrate the church regarding our **people** is to shift the starting point of our churches from the *fourth place* back to the neighborhood.

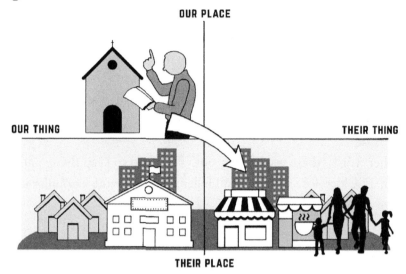

In this chapter we are talking about **people,** so you'll notice some people have been added to the chart. The preacher lives in OUR THING, OUR PLACE—the church building, the *fourth place*. On the opposite corner we have a family. They live in THEIR THING, THEIR PLACE, otherwise known as normal life.

A Separate Religious Class

Our leadership is what it is today because it is based in the *fourth place*. As we saw back in Chapter 4, church shifted from a spiritual family to an event. Church changed from a WHO to a WHAT. When Constantine separated the church from culture, he stole people out of normal life and made them church specialists.

Not only did the leaders lose touch with how to shepherd people through real life, but the new size expectations put pastors in the middle of a no-win situation.

Pastor Catch-22

Joseph Heller wrote a sadly humorous book called *Catch-22*. The main character, Captain John Yossarian, along with his fellow airmen in the war, were in a no-win situation. Flying combat missions was extremely dangerous and every mission represented another chance to die. The only way to get out of flying was to be deemed crazy; however, to claim oneself as crazy was declared a sane act since it was acting in self-preservation.

In other words, there was no way out. They had to keep flying and risk death. The lose-lose situation in Heller's book became a popular idiom known as a catch-22.

Pastors find themselves in a type of catch-22. The only way to pastor people is to know them deeply. This requires understanding their world. This also requires pastoring only a small number of people. Jesus chose twelve and only three were in his inner-circle. However, the only way to pay the bills and survive as a pastor is to have a lot of people in the congregation.

In other words, our event-based definition of church is forcing pastors to maintain a size of congregation that is impossible to actually pastor.

It's a catch-22, a no-win situation. Like Yossarian, most pastors are financially forced to keep flying. Sadly, many of them are dying spiritually, flaming out, getting depressed or failing morally.

Pastors often go into the "ministry" wanting to help people's souls but eventually realize they simply don't have time to know people at that level. Eventually, pastors give up on shepherding people and default to preaching good sermons—that is, if they have the talent.

After all, Sunday's always coming!

Sidetracked

by Dudley Callison

I was a "lead pastor" for a couple of years at a delightful little church. At first, I enjoyed being known as their pastor. A year later, I questioned what that even meant. I spent most of the week creating a sermon and planning the Sunday event. I had little time to be with the people. Honestly, even though my title was "Pastor," my real job was as a professional orator and event planner. And forget spending time with people who didn't yet know Jesus. I barely had time to meet with key church leaders, who were also focused on the upcoming weekly gathering.

After leaving that church, I began serving in a ministry focused on at-risk teens. That community didn't know me as a church leader. I think this actually helped them to trust me. In fact, looking back I can say that I really began to "pastor" others after I left the official role. Helping people walk toward Jesus is at the heart of the pastoral life, and no title or job description should keep us from that central task.

One of our Communitas churches, Sampa Church, began in Sao Paulo, Brazil when a lovely Christian couple relocated from Amsterdam. Neither person was a seminary trained, ordained pastor. The husband worked for Rolls Royce! They met some other believers who also wanted to gather and enjoy an English-speaking church. As they met, they listened to CDs or Podcasts. The work of the "pastor" was not to teach, but to shepherd people toward applying what they had heard. The great irony is that once this couple was free of the traditional "pastor" job description they were finally able to pastor people.

The situation is just as bad for the congregation. People come to a church wanting a spiritual guide, and eventually realize the pastor doesn't have time for them. He or she only has time to counsel a few people in crisis. The only way to get any attention is to be in crisis or be a super-volunteer, spending all of one's time at the church building. Eventually, people give up on the pastor ever being able to truly shepherd their soul or even care about their day-to-day life. They settle for being entertained by sermons—that is, until they aren't very entertaining any more. That's when it's off to greener pastures to find someone who will "feed" them better.

It's a catch-22. It isn't working. In our current model, pastors can't shepherd souls. People don't have a guide to help them through life. Pastors are stuck as event planners, and the rest of us are forced to consume sermon after sermon.

While Heller's book is a page turner and absolutely hilarious, the catch-22 our pastors are stuck in is a tragedy. We are to be a living picture of the reconciliation of all things—integration with God, with each other and with the world itself. We need to know how to work jobs faithfully, how to love people who are hard to love, how to pray for our neighbors. We need our leaders to model these things. Pastoral ministry needs to be more about spiritual formation than public oration.

"Pastoral ministry needs to be more about spiritual formation than public oration."

The function of the church is to learn how to live a redeemed life in the midst of culture. We cannot learn this from someone whose whole world represents separation. We cannot learn how to seek the peace of our city from someone consumed by maintaining the *fourth place*. This is why we need to completely redefine the word *pastor*.

Pastor Redefined

The pastoral job description became what it is because of the trajectory set by its starting point. The key to redefining this vital role is to uproot our old foundation and rebuild on Christ's foundation.

Constantine's foundational paradigm is this: **Church is primarily an event in a building.** If church is an event, then the leader of the church is primarily an event planner. But we have a better foundation—**church is a spiritual family.** Church is a WHO, not a WHAT. And if church is a family, then the leaders of the family are not event planners, but fathers and mothers.

Paul said it like this, "Even if you had ten thousand guardians in Christ, you do not have many fathers, for in Christ Jesus I became your father through the gospel. Therefore I urge you to imitate me" (1 Cor. 4:15-16). Peter tells elders to be "examples to the flock" (1 Peter 5:3). How, then, do we change from being professional orators and event planners to becoming living examples? How do we transition off the stage to become fathers and mothers?

A New Definition

If we want to see leadership in the church that enables pastors to actually shepherd souls within culture, three key movements are needed in our basic understanding of the word *pastor*: **event-based to family-based, professional to amateur** and **isolated to networked.**

1. Event-Based to Family-Based

Go to any pastor conference and the dreaded question, "How's your church doing?" can only mean one thing: "How many people are showing up on Sunday?" Success for the modern pastor is tied directly to numbers because event planners measure success by event metrics—attendance and event-satisfaction.

When we change from being event planners to being shepherds, the metrics change. Mothers and fathers see their families very differently than event planners see their events. Mothers and fathers know they can best impact the world by investing deeply in a few children. They are not looking for big numbers but deep relationships.

In chapter 9, we talked about the impact the Ufitzi Missional Order is making in Santa Barbara, California. The homeless and the affluent come together to learn from one another. The leaders sit on civil councils where they are able to help their city seek justice for women stuck in the sex trade. However, at their core are twelve people. They are a small spiritual family. They do not define themselves by a gathering, but by an agreed upon way of life in community.

Families come in all shapes and sizes. They can be a small nuclear family of three or an enormous extended family of fifty. Mothers and fathers are not trying to make a big crowd happy, but walk with their kids through all of life's many ups and down. If we are going to redefine the pastor role, we need to shift from event-based leadership to family-based leadership.

2. Professional to Amateur

The second key change to the definition of the word *pastor* is a decrease in specialization. In order to do this, we must shift the focus to the family meal rather than the family wedding. An Iranian immigrant is equipped to start a new church gathering because a family meal requires no specialization in its leadership. The elements of the event are something an amateur could do—dinner, discussion around scripture, singing where anyone could play along, community prayer time and fellowship.

Jesus did not leave us a wedding to remember him by; he left us a family meal. On the night he was betrayed, they ate bread and drank wine together. Jesus talked about his body and blood. There was conversation, even arguing about who was the greatest. Normal life was happening! That's the beauty of a meal. Jesus said to do this family meal over and over again in order to remember him until he returns. It was simple, doable, reproducible, culturally transferable. Every culture has families. Every culture eats. In this way, the church could reproduce itself into every culture of the world. Temple structures ask people to conform. Jesus' structure allowed the kingdom to move freely amongst every culture and subculture of the world without destroying the beauty of the world's diversity.

There is no right way to do a family meal. We have seen examples of the community meal from Jesus in Judea, Paul in Corinth, Justin Martyr in Rome, and Tertullian in North Africa. All the gatherings were different. Church should be as full of variety as the various cultures it represents. There is also continuity. In each case, the gospel of Jesus is central and church is an *all-play*. Everyone takes part in the meal, the word, the prayers, the giving. There are clear leadership roles—an overseer, deacons, a reader—but they move in and among the community, not over and above it. This is the **integration of people**. This is church, a community of equals.

Upper Room Glasgow looks very similar to these ancient gatherings. What was done two thousand years ago in Hebrew, Aramaic or Greek is working for Iranian immigrants speaking Farsi in Scotland. It still works. No professionals are required. If we are going to integrate our **people**, we must de-professionalize the role of the pastor.

Is this the only gathering size that works for a church? No, but it is the foundation. A community can be enormous and can include large gatherings of thousands, but at its core will be a network of spiritual families. A church can do without large worship services, but they cannot do without a place to experience real life in community.

3. Isolated to Networked

I recently had a conversation with Dave Runyon, coauthor of the book, *The Art of Neighboring*. His organization gathers pastors regionally to help them connect and work together to better their communities. He told me that as he meets with pastor after pastor, he hears the same story over and over—senior pastors have no friends. They are isolated. Power dynamics keep them from honest friendships in their own congregations, and they don't have time or space in their lives for anyone else. Besides, their day off (if they even have one) is opposite the rest of the world.

This is a problem. Isolation is contributing to pastoral depression and moral failure. It is keeping pastors from cooperating with other pastors. Not only that, but isolation is causing the church to miss out on many of the gifts that the New Testament offers us, especially those known as APEPT or APEST—Apostles, Prophets, Evangelists, Pastors (Shepherds) and Teachers. For the most part we can only afford to pay for one—the pastor/teacher role. Of course, larger churches can hire large staffs, but how many of these churches are really hiring apostles and prophets and evangelists? For the most part, they are hiring communication directors, video producers, human resources and facilities managers, and many more internal-facing roles. For most churches, all hiring points to the building, and the senior pastor is simply the CEO over all facility and event operations.

The reality is that we are utilizing few of the APEPT gifts because all of our resources are tied up running events in buildings. Rather than empowering everyone as participants in a great decentralized kingdom movement, we are simply making our big-name pastors even bigger. The satellite campus movement is not helping the situation. While making the star pastor more visible to the masses, the multiplication of video-venues simply extends the reach of one super-talented leader even further.

If we are going to have any sense of unity or cooperation in the church, the power dynamics simply must change. An integrated church model accomplishes this. When pastors are fathers and mothers rather than event planners, they are looking for deep relationships rather than big numbers. In this way, the other gifts from APEPT are released. If you are multiplying smaller communities you need people to coordinate the network as a whole. You need apostolic leaders to break new ground and provide vision. You need prophetic leaders to listen to God, pray, and challenge the individual communities toward a bigger vision. You need teachers to train new leaders and equip the pastors for their ministry.

Consider the example of Young Life. A Young Life Area Director will tell their leaders and staff, "If you want to work closely with kids, be a volunteer. If you want to get paid, be an Area Director, but anticipate a lot of paperwork and less hands-on ministry with kids." Area Directors are like apostles. They don't use this title, but that is their function. They are the glue—the relational leaders who keep all of the local volunteers and staff coordinated and moving forward. If we are going to allow pastors to finally pastor people, we are going to need a strong APEPT network around them.

The definition of the word pastor needs to change. From event-based to family-based, professional to amateur, and isolated to networked. In order to do this, one of the biggest hurdles that must be overcome is money. There is a good reason we only focus on one gift in the Western church. We can't afford to pay for the rest! In order to move toward an integrated church, we must address our deeply rooted and broken financial model.

Fee-for-Service

The primary financial model used in the Western church is the fee-for-service model.

I was talking to a senior pastor friend a few days ago who told me about several recent conversations with members of his congregation. He has been attempting to raise up a preaching team in order to share the preaching load and train young preachers. His efforts, however, have not all been appreciated by his congregation. Several members have asked him,"If you are not preaching every week, then what are we paying you for?"

The fee-for-service financial model says, "If you preach well and grow the church then we will keep paying your salary through our tithes." Underlying this idea is an outsourcing model of ministry. The main ministry tasks—preaching, weddings and funerals—are all outsourced to the paid professionals. The more important the ministry task, the more money we pay. Senior pastors make a living wage, associates a little less, administrators less still. Human resources literature will tell you that larger church pastors should make more than smaller church pastors. It is simple economics, supply and demand. Supply a good product that demands more attendance and tithe contributions, and you deserve more money.

Regardless of polity, whether Congregational, Presbyterian, or otherwise, most Western churches use a fee-for-service financial model. We pay professional ministry people for religious services rendered.

Should people who preach and teach God's word be paid? Yes. But how much? Paul writes to Timothy, "The elders who direct the affairs of the church well are worthy of double honor, especially those whose work is preaching and teaching" (1 Tim 5:17). How much were they really getting paid? These were small communities. These were people with other sources of income who were devoting part of their life to overseeing a church. These were not professional orators on stages performing for thousands. Preaching did not mean delivering a polished speech; it meant reading scripture out loud and explaining it. It meant telling stories about Jesus and leading a community discussion.[74] They received some compensation to honor their time and effort, but this was a stipend, not a salary. The goal of these elders was to give ministry away, not to get paid to do it all themselves.

That is why Paul teaches us, "So Christ himself gave the apostles, the prophets, the evangelists, the pastors and teachers, to equip his people for works of service, so that the body of Christ may be built up" (Eph. 4:11-12).

We make disciples by releasing real responsibility to others, not by outsourcing it to the professionals. Mutual participation in the ministry is the key to everyone's growth. If you want to understand why we are raising up a culture of spiritual infants and consumers, we need to understand that it is directly related to our broken financial model.

Empowered Participant Leadership

An integrated church flips the fee-for-service model on its head. Rather than outsourcing ministry to a few professionals, an integrated church empowers as many people as possible to contribute to the community and mission, regardless of pay. Here is an example:

A newly married couple named Josh and Lucía are leading a church in Spain. Josh is a singer-songwriter and Lucía is a gifted painter. They

---

[74] McGowan, *Ancient Christian Worship*, 73-75.

live in an extremely diverse and artistic district of Madrid called Malasaña. Like all Communitas church planters, Josh and Lucía began with WHO, not WHAT. They studied their culture, built relationships and prayed, and God opened up an opportunity to now help lead a beautiful community of people who call themselves Decoupage.

One way they have embedded themselves into the fabric of Malasaña is by opening a coworking business designed specifically for artists. They lease space to both Christian and non-Christian artists for a fraction of what normal artistic spaces would cost. Not only do they run a business, but they use their art to bless the neighborhood. Every year, they research a need in the community and create a giant mural (Lucía's specialty). They write a question on an urban wall and allow the neighborhood to write their responses. This annual tradition has gained Decoupage an enormous amount of respect in the community.

Decoupage is much more than a mere worship service. They meet in homes and apartments to share meals, song and prayer, and they also share life and mission outside their gatherings. They do not impose their own goals on the neighborhood, but listen for real needs and then actively work together to meet those needs. Lucía teaches art lessons for local kids, including the very poor. One of the moms so appreciated Lucía's investment in her child that she opened up to her about her own need for work as well as her questions about God. She and Lucía began studying the Bible together. The community helped this woman write a résumé and get a job. When it came time for her daughter's birthday, this mom could not afford a party so the entire Decoupage community threw her a celebration she would never forget. This family has now come to Christ and joined the community.

Decoupage is a living picture of the reconciliation of all three spheres of relationships. They are growing closer to God. They are living in loving community. They are using their artistic gifts to make the world more beautiful and interesting. They are seeking the peace of their city. Josh and Lucía only receive a small amount of their income from church giving—400 euros a month to be exact. The majority of the giving goes right back into the needs of the neighborhood.

Josh and Lucía are part of a new church financial model. In this system, the goal is not to support a church facility and the people who run the programs of that facility. That would be to remove disciple makers from their natural cultural context. Instead, the goal is to keep people within culture where they are able to reach and develop new disciples of Jesus.

When you start from the building, you need someone to run the building. You need someone to run the programs of the building. You need high specialization. Professional Christians are expensive. Buildings, utilities and maintenance are expensive. Therefore you need a large body of tithing individuals to keep the machine running.

When you start from culture, everything changes. No building. No utilities. No professionals. Therefore, the financial model can work differently.

Communitas and other church planting networks support a wide array of financial arrangements. Some church planters and pastors are supported full-time by the generosity of their communities. Some are supported through donor development (fundraising). Many aren't. Many are bankers, or artists, or managers who also pastor a small spiritual family. They receive their paychecks from their employer, not from a church planting network. Some call this arrangement bi-vocational, but that term is often used to speak of pastors who have not yet "succeeded" enough in ministry size and tithe income to receive full-time support. This view of bi-vocational is not true of how Communitas views ministry and money. Success is not equated with full-time support. In fact, it is often just the opposite.

If you talked to Josh and Lucía they would tell you that their financial arrangement is beneficial for a number of reasons:

1. They like how running a business and pastoring a smaller community keeps them free from the mixed motives that come from the fee-for-service model.

2. They know that in Spain, answering the question, "What do you do?" with "I'm a Pastor" will kill the conversation before it even starts. Lucía is glad she can honestly say, "I am an artist. I run a business."

3. They love the fact that by not being on a paid staff, it invites other people in the community to naturally step up and take ownership of the ministry.

4. They appreciate and lean on the support they receive from the Communitas network.

Josh and Lucía love being a part of a community that isn't constantly self-promoting and overusing its volunteers. According to Josh, who has used his musical talents to serve in other churches in the past, "This is the first church I truly believe in. It is hard and frustrating work at times, but I can finally sleep well at night."

Josh and Lucía are walking alongside others in spiritual family, not above them on a platform. Everyone takes part. Everyone has gifts, passions and a voice. Some of their fellow artists are teachers. Some have gifts of mercy and compassion. Others are gifted in hospitality. Lucía is more of an evangelist. Josh is more pastoral.

Having a team allows them to focus where they are more gifted.

In addition, beyond their own team and community they are supported by a much larger network. Communitas leaders don't go around trumpeting, "I am an apostle," or "I am a prophet," as if these were badges of honor. However, in every way their network functions both apostolically and prophetically. Josh and Lucía aren't alone. They have people within Communitas leadership to help them continue to dream about God's heart for Malasaña. They have people listening to God with them for the sake of their city. On the other side of town lives a Communitas couple that takes time to care for their souls. They meet together regularly for prayer and mentoring. They attend global and local conferences where they form lasting relationships with others around the world in positions similar to theirs. They participate in local learning communities which have become a vital source of encouragement and training.

Many of these apostolic and prophetic leaders receive full-time or part-time pay from Communitas. They are the relational and operational glue behind the scenes. They are listening to God. They are strategizing new ground to break. They are training and releasing new leaders.

If you were concerned at the idea of de-professionalizing the pastoral role, I want to assure you that following this course does not lead to a lack of theologically trained people within the network. It simply means that Josh and Lucía don't need all of that training for themselves. The network of gifts removes the pressure. It allows pastors to be normal humans that God can use to love and disciple a few people.

Whereas many pastors feel alone at the top, Josh and Lucía feel like they are part of a network—a global community of people of various gifts all sharing the same mission. This is the integration of **people.** No mountains and no valleys. No clergy elevated above the laity. Equal participation.

No celebrity personas needed.

The End of the Christian Celebrity

Where are the heroes in this network? Where are the big names? Are they the people at the top with the big titles? No, nobody even knows who they are. They office at coffee shops and coworking spaces. They work tirelessly for the sake of the mission but their faces don't show up on any billboards.

Pastors are normal humans who love a few people really well. They are multiplying big lives, not big crowds. They are extraordinary in the little things, the ordinary. When a church grows toward a size where the leader could become a celebrity, that is the time they are most likely to plant another church.

In an integrated church, the hero is not the big voice on the stage. Often there is no stage or microphone. The hero is the person working their job faithfully and sharing life with a few people. The hero is the person sharing a meal with a neighbor. The hero is spending yet another hour on their knees in prayer. The hero is doing what they should be doing— living like Christ. Jesus said, "The Son of Man did not come to be served, but to serve, and to give his life as a ransom for many" (Matt. 20:28).

Our modern phenomenon of big stages and satellite campuses makes sense in the Western world. If we have something great, we want everybody to experience it. We want to spread it. If we have a successful product, the cultural narrative tells us to maximize it at all costs.

When we do this, don't we just become another Constantine? He created a standardized model of church and then spread it throughout the world. I'm sure he thought that his beautiful basilica was just what the people living in Bethlehem needed. He probably wasn't thinking, "You know what, Judeans are different from Romans. We should take the slow and long path of raising up local Judean leaders and working within their existing architecture." No, he didn't have time for that! He had something that was working, so he built Rome right on top of the manger.

Isn't that us today? Isn't that the satellite movement? We don't have time for slow growth either. We want to spread our successful church culture while the iron is hot. We all want to be heroes, but that just isn't the path of Jesus. Until we leave the *fourth place*, we will be stuck as anxious self-promoters and event planners. Our paycheck will be connected to drawing crowds. We will be jealous of the "successful" pastors with the big churches.

If it is any encouragement to you, there are celebrity leaders making the hard choice to forego the adulation of the crowds for a simpler way of church. Francis Chan tells the story of preaching to crowds of thousands all the while feeling guilty for wasting God's precious resources. He had a church of five thousand people and realized each of them was empowered to do kingdom work. Many of them were running successful companies, but because they were partaking in his definition of megachurch, they were just sitting in a large room and listening to the guy on stage. It was costing millions of dollars, taking enormous amounts of time, and the fruit was a room full of onlookers, not participants.[75] Chan is now running a house church network called We Are Church. It is organized around empowering many leaders to shepherd small communities of active participants and self-feeders.

I applaud Chan. This is a risky and humbling move not many leaders are willing to make.

---

[75]Francis Chan: "Why I Left the Megachurch I Created!" YouTube video, 9:43, Francis Chan answering questions live on Facebook, posted by Keith Thompson, accessed October 27, 2017, https://www.youtube.com/watch?v=KQ9Yeq-tavk.

Jesus' path leads to the cross, not the stage. It is time to decrease the size, remove the complexity, and allow a network of loving and gifted people to serve our cities together. It is time to get off the platform and into the neighborhood. It is time to integrate our **people** and make church an *all-play*.

"Jesus' path leads to the cross, not the stage."

Hope for the Established Church

I understand that this model of church can feel pretty different from what many of us are used to. I also understand that participating in a fundamentally different wineskin of church isn't an option for all of us. Our denomination, our polity, our financial model, our culture of senior pastors on the stage are too deeply ingrained to make that type of change right now.

If you are coming from an existing building-based church, there are many ways that you can incrementally move toward the integration of **people** without selling your building. No matter where you are starting right now, you can take tangible steps toward the leveling of your leadership and the empowering of your people.

Let me offer you a challenge. The temptation in the *fourth place* is always to simply try to grow the event even bigger. Maybe that's you right now. You are getting pressure to preach better, hire a better worship leader or use better technology. But as most of us know by now, we will never quite get there. We will always need just a few more tithing units, a couple more staff and some better gear. In the end we are simply producing bigger leaders and smaller consumer Christians.

If you are ready to get off the *fourth place* hamster wheel, here are three very practical directions you can move instead:

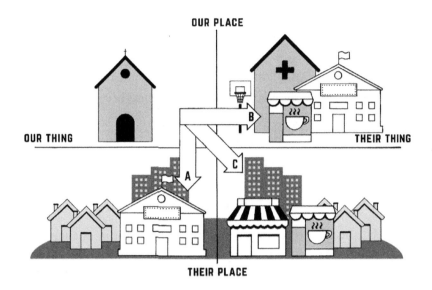

A. OUR THING, THEIR PLACE

In order to blur the lines between clergy and laity, there is no more proven way than a great small groups program. If your church can release more pastoral care and responsibility to a group of leaders in homes, you have gone a long way toward integrating **people**. Not only do people in groups get the pastoral care they long for, but the celebrity persona is no longer the primary glue that connects people to your church. The glue becomes relationships—spiritual family.

B. THEIR THING, OUR PLACE

Part of the church moving away from the holy celebrity persona is simply helping your leaders learn how to exist like normal humans again. If you can make your church building into a legitimate *first, second* or *third place* for your neighborhood, this makes a big difference. Even though your church staff still offices in the building, they are regularly rubbing shoulders with the patrons of the coffee shop or the tech startup team officing out of your coworking space. All of a sudden they are interacting with the normal flow of life and stories of your neighbors instead of the constant barrage of churchgoers. This reconnection to reality shifts their whole way of thinking, preaching and practicing ministry in the community. In addition, when these valued tenants and businesspeople experience good relationships with your staff and other Christians, it builds a natural bridge to your faith community. People who are normally hesitant to attend church might actually take the risk of joining a small group or walking through your doors on a Sunday morning.

C. THEIR THING, THEIR PLACE

Ultimately, the goal is to get people to live like Christ in their world. One of the reasons we are not making disciples is that people think Christianity is about sitting in a row and observing professional Christians. Before people will take real risks for Christ in their world you will need to help people move from the posture of observer to participant. How can you do this?

Does your church do service projects in the community? Use these not just as ends in themselves but as exposure events that get people to care about the needs in their own neighborhood. Ask people the question, "What if you did this type of work for the people in your own life"? Provide easy ways for people to take steps in their own world, their own neighborhoods and coworkers.

What if you created an environment for some basic missional training, dialogue and a place to dream and pray together for where to start? Help empower people to take the initiative with some friends in their own world. Don't plan everything for them from the church center. Let people take the lead, make mistakes and learn on their own. Sit in circles instead of rows whenever possible. Come alongside them as a coach and friend.

Remember, this type of culture shift will not happen through sermons alone. You will need to create environments, whether in small groups or at the building, to allow people a place to cultivate what Alan Roxborough calls their *missional imagination*.[76] Changing fundamental posture from observer to participant is challenging. Don't expect to see the entire church change right away. Be thankful for a few early adopters that can start to build momentum for others through their stories. If you invest the time and prayer, and your leadership team owns the change for their own lives, you will see God's incarnational heart grow in your people.

Changing the Culture of the Fourth Place

In addition to the three directions we just talked about, there are positive ways for churches to practice the integration of people even within the *fourth place*. Many churches are utilizing a preaching team instead of one primary voice. This creates less dependence on one person and releases more people into their gifts.

Another way to slowly shift your culture is to allow more time for personal stories on your stage. Simply allowing non-trained people a chance to share about their lives and spiritual journeys in Christ helps to demythologize the stage. Video testimonies are fine, but the whole point of video editing as a medium is to clean up and polish people. The medium itself removes us a step from reality. In order to practice a better Christology where human and divine exist together, we need to allow unpolished people to be themselves.

Other ways to integrate people involve changes to the service itself. Some churches are experimenting with people sitting at round tables instead of rows. They are allowing for discussion in their services instead of the usual monologue. Others are celebrating a less formal

---

[76] Roxburgh and Boren, *Introducing the Missional Church*.

Eucharist. People leave their seats and pray with others. All of these changes are small shifts away from the liturgy of the wedding toward the liturgy of the family meal. Leaders become more human and attendees become participants. In all of these small changes the medium begins to reflect a better message of equality in our **people**.

Onto the Integration of Our Practices

We have now integrated two of our three forms. We've discussed the integration of **place**, and we've seen what integration of **people** looks like. But we're not done yet. If we integrate **place** and **people**, but keep our idea that growth happens primarily from singing and sermons, we will likely fail. It's time to redefine worship. It's time to integrate our **practices**.

11

Holistic Worship

I went to college at the University of Puget Sound in Tacoma, Washington. As a freshman I didn't know what to expect and was pretty nervous as I entered my new world for the next four years. That fall a senior invited me to a retreat on the ocean with a campus ministry called Lighthouse. I went and it quite literally changed my life forever. I had never seen anything like that community before—the way they loved God and each other. I had found a new home.

Before college I didn't have many honest friendships. Through Lighthouse I got connected to a small group of six other freshman guys who could talk about anything. We studied the Bible and asked big questions about God and life late into the night. We supported each other as we tried our best to figure out the opposite sex. We served the homeless together in the greater city of Tacoma.

I didn't realize it at the time, but in college I experienced a taste of an integrated church. We were a spiritual family on mission together. We were deeply dedicated to our campus, and not just the basement where a hundred and fifty or so of us gathered every week. We lived on campus. We ate there. We played frisbee golf there. We made ridiculous movies there. The University of Puget Sound is one of the most liberal universities in the country, yet we lived right in the middle of a very challenging environment as followers of Jesus in exile.

The campus was our mini-city and we sought its peace together. As we did, we saw the hand of God at work. We saw lives changed. Drunken frat boys became lovers of God. Porn addicts experienced true freedom from their addictions. Women full of shame from past abuse or rape gained a new identity and confidence as children of God. Rich suburban kids grew to love the inner city of Tacoma. Through all of this a question lingered: "Is this just a college ministry thing or could a community live like this in the *real world?*"

We took up the challenge. A group of us, guys and girls, continued to meet together after graduation. We weren't going to be like those adults who lose their passion for life and God through isolation and consumerism. We were going to live differently. More people joined our community. We picked a theme verse for our mission having to do with salt. We were going to keep each other salty—able to make an impact on our world of new careers and families. We jokingly called our little group, NaCl (*Nackle*), the molecular symbol for salt. Yes, our group contained more than its fair share of science geeks! Somehow the name stuck.

Eventually, inspired by some mentors of ours and some books we were reading together (thank you, John Lewis and Randy Frazee!) we felt compelled to move into a neighborhood together where we would not only keep each other salty in our separate lives, but also experience shared life and purpose among our neighbors.

We wanted to stick together, so we found careers that would keep us local. I worked at Russell Investments, headquartered in Tacoma. Ben taught high school science and coached cross country. Pam worked for REACH, an organization dedicated to the HIV/AIDS community. Jason went off to Stanford for his MBA, and returned to work as an executive at Da Vita, a leader in kidney dialysis. Spanning the worlds of for-profit, non-profit, education and more, our neighborhood community made us more like Jesus in our workplaces.

We met weekly in the neighborhood for a meal and Bible study; more than that, we shared all of life. Spontaneity was the norm. People randomly showed up in our backyard to jump on our trampoline or just hang out.

We encouraged each other's marriages and parenting. We saw first hand the benefit of our kids growing up with a whole network of friends and adults they could trust. One of the kids has CHARGE syndrome and is unable to hear and speak, yet she has a whole group of kids using sign language with her.

Community was not always easy. Conflicts came up and needed to be resolved. There were differences of opinion that needed to be discussed. That's how it should be. That is how families work. Through this experience I got to taste what it means to live as an integrated church, a spiritual family on mission together. What we experienced in college on campus, we experienced in the bigger city of Tacoma.

And we saw fruit. In our own lives. In our kids. In my middle-school neighbor whose dad walked out on him. We started by just playing catch in the backyard. Eventually, he went off to college to become a youth pastor. We saw God working in his sister, who was cutting her arms with razor blades. One night we got to take her out to buy her first Bible in celebration of her finding hope in Christ. We even saw God working in the teachers that came to our group and cried with us as they thanked us for investing in their school with them. We sought God's peace in our neighborhood and we saw God's peace come.

Today the community is still going strong, still investing in each other, still making an impact on the neighborhood. I miss it terribly. Nine years ago, sensing God's leading, my family and I headed to Colorado and Denver Seminary. I wanted to better understand why most Christians never taste what it's like to be part of a spiritual family. I wanted to study how a biblical ecclesiology can and should inform how we practice church. What I studied there, along with many other conversations, books and experiences, helped form what you are reading.

I hope it has been a meaningful journey for you. We have walked through the Garden of Eden, past the Old Testament temple, into the life of Christ, through fourth century Rome, and finally to the modern Western church. We have looked at the forms of **place, people** and **practices** as they have developed historically and how our history still impacts us today. We have begun to build the framework of an integrated church, one whose form matches its function. In this, the last chapter, we now arrive at our final medium, **practices**.

I saved this one for last because it follows naturally from the other two. In other words, unless you also integrate **place** and **people**, it is very difficult to integrate **practices**. The basic principle of an integrated church regarding **practices** is this: **the church worships as we live connected to God in all spheres of life.**

Our community in Tacoma experienced a taste of holistic worship. Unfortunately, the current model of *fourth place* church has made holistic worship unattainable for many believers. Instead of living sacrificially for one another, we are using a paradigm of church that puts all the sacrifice—our time, talents, and resources—into the *fourth place*. How do we change this? How do we let go of our physical temple attachment and give ourselves instead to the living temple within culture?

Once again, our starting point is the issue. In order to see lasting change to the way we approach Christian **practices**, we must address our foundation. We must rebuild the temple on a foundation of people rather than religious events. We must come out of the *fourth place* and return the church to where it belongs.

Again, this chart is helpful for understanding both the problem *and* the solution.

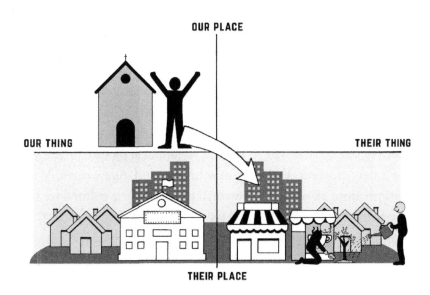

Since we're talking about worship, I added a little worshiping person to OUR THING, OUR PLACE. This is what many people think of when they hear the word *worship*. Standing and praising God is a beautiful thing, but it is only a small part of the worship Jesus came to give us.

THEIR THING, THEIR PLACE is where people eat, sleep, work and live. It is the only quadrant that would have existed if not for Eden's fall, so I added some happy gardening people. As Tim Keller suggests, all meaningful work, whether medicine, construction, the arts, or teaching ultimately points back to the cultivation of God's original materials.[77] In other words, all of us are at some level, gardeners. All of us are still called to steward God's good, but tainted, creation.

Rehearsing for the Wrong Eternity

I have often heard it argued that since we will be worshipping God forever and ever, why not practice now by running great worship services? "Worship is a rehearsal for eternity," they say. While many people express this sentiment with a great heart, there is a problem with the logic. Here is the issue: most of our churches have been rehearsing for a *fourth place* view of eternity.

Our event-focused "rehearsal" assumes that heaven is an eternal worship service. While Revelation has some beautiful images of worship in song around the throne, as N.T. Wright argues, that is not a picture of our eternal state.[78] Rather, the biblical picture of eternity is one of a new creation. We see a new heaven and a new earth. We see the nations from all over the new earth bringing their cultural treasures into a great city (Rev. 21:24). We see new trees of life (Rev. 22:2). We see people coming and going in and out of the city whose gates will never be shut (Rev. 21:25-26).

We don't see any description of an eternal worship service. Instead, we see a garden-city. This is not an escape from our humanity, but humanity 2.0. This is not a retirement in the clouds, but a promotion to even more responsibility.

Producing cultural treasures (Rev. 21:24) implies meaningful work. Building things implies that there will be craftsmanship and art.

---

[77] Timothy Keller. "Work: Cultivating the Garden." Session 6. *Gospel in Life* DVD. Grand Rapids: Zondervan Curriculum, 2010.
[78] N.T. Wright, *Surprised by Hope: Rethinking Heaven, the Resurrection, and the Mission of the Church* (New York: Harper Collins, 2008).

Moving things around implies transportation. If Jesus said he eagerly awaits celebrating with bread and wine in the coming kingdom (Matt. 26:29), there must be the farming of wheat and the cultivation of grapevines. As Randy Alcorn in his book, *Heaven*, suggests, if there is grape production, why shouldn't there be coffee bean production?[79] Okay, I'm from Seattle and I'm counting on eternity to include great coffee!

The new heaven and new earth are a place for us to finally understand what it means to be human. When heaven and earth are at last married, we will finally get to see our original purpose on the earth fulfilled, to steward God's good creation. We practice for heaven not through endless worship services, but by living holistic kingdom lives now. God has given us a garden. It is full of weeds, but it has potential. And we are the gardeners.

The Cutting Edge of Worship

People are always wondering what the next movement in worship is going to be. In the 1980s, many churches pushed toward "contemporary worship." They added electric guitars and drums; they started raising their hands and dancing. In the 1990s, they moved toward bigger production with smoke machines, expensive lighting, video, stage design and TV production. In the 2000s they pushed satellite campuses and online churches. Other churches, some as a reaction to the megachurch show, have moved toward church forms that feel more ancient. There is a push for more liturgy—more "smells and bells."

With this pattern, what is the next big thing in worship? DJ-led worship? Hip hop worship? Another art medium? More liturgy?

---

[79] Randy Alcorn, *Heaven* (Carol Stream, Il: Tyndale House Publishers, inc., 2004).

What if we are just as confused about worship as the woman at the well? What if, like this woman, we are still asking questions about temple worship while Jesus is trying to open our minds and hearts to a whole new paradigm of life in the Spirit? What if the next movement of worship isn't another *fourth place* fad? What if it is a movement toward real life—holistic worship? What if it is a movement toward lives of radical mercy in community?

Worship in Exile

Worship looks different in exile than in a temple. We aren't called to maintain a building anymore. We are called to be a *living* building, cultivating God's garden.

For the Uffizi Missional Order in Santa Barbara, worship isn't about singing songs. It's about collaborating with seventeen other organizations in order to effectively feed hundreds of "friends without homes" in Pershing Park. It's about working with the city council to effect change in the sex trade.

For Josh and Lucía in Madrid, worship is about providing art classes to impoverished kids. It is looking after another elderly person with cancer. It is listening carefully and patiently to one another to discern each other's gifts and how God might want to use them.

For our Nackle community in Tacoma, the city was our garden. Our careers were given in worship to God. Our work at the local neighborhood elementary school was our sacrifice. Our participation in the all-neighborhood garage sale was an annual liturgy. Every time we walked to each other's homes to gather, it was a sacred procession. Our meals together were communion. Our prayers were the natural outflow of a community that loved each other. It didn't matter how beautiful our songs were. Kids and adults sang along together, praising God for his goodness that we got to experience in community.

We had an annual retreat where all of our families would get away to the mountains and rent one huge house. We would share meals, play all day, jump in the river, play games at night, and come to God together around a campfire. One day the men would watch all of the kids so the women could go get some girl time. The next day the women would watch the kids and the men would go do something stupid together where one of us would always get injured. I broke my friend Jon's nose once playing some ridiculous version of football that guys our age should never play.

Was community always wonderful? Of course not. Sometimes it was pretty messy and frustrating. But it was real. Worship was holistic. All three spheres of relationships were at once being redeemed and formed by our God. We walked together to encourage each other toward a deepening love of God. We worked hard to build supportive relationships with each other. We processed together our own gifts and callings so that we could maximize each other's contributions to the world.

We experienced communion with God, community with each other and mission and work in the world. Worship and life were one.

An Immersion Experience

Do you want to experience church like this? I know I do.

Our world needs to see a church that can walk humbly in community with each other, a church that practices mercy and uses its resources to love its neighbors, a church where the world can tell we are Christians by our love for one another.

How do we move away from a focus on maintaining a building and shift toward cultivating the garden God has called us to steward? We're going to get really practical in this next section.

But first, I want to offer a challenge concerning our paradigm of growth. For many of us, discipleship is so attached to the building that we have a hard time imagining anything other than sermons and classes. To stretch our imaginations, I want you to consider a different growth paradigm—immersion.

Consider the example of language learning. We all know that the best way to learn a language is immersion within that culture. We can take two years of classes in Spanish and not learn as much as spending a month or two in Spain or Mexico. Immersion is a far better teacher than a series of classroom lectures. This is also true in most other areas of growth, whether physical, emotional or spiritual.

In Matthew 13, Jesus tells the crowds the parable of the sower. A farmer went out and cast seeds in different types of soil. One type of soil produced a lot of growth and therefore a lot of fruit—one hundred, sixty or thirty times what was planted. The crowds were confused. The disciples were confused. Jesus pulled his disciples away from the crowds and then explained it to them in private. He told them that the secrets of the kingdom had been given to them (disciples), but to the crowds he was speaking in parables.

Why in the world would Jesus intentionally use confusing language with the crowds? Why not just speak clearly? This passage always bothered me until I understood the power of immersion growth. What if the *secrets of the kingdom* were things like suffering, love, mercy or service? There are some things that you can't learn in a crowd who shows up for a little while and then goes home. The *secrets of the kingdom* are for people who join Jesus in his kingdom immersion experience.

It's not that Jesus didn't want to tell them. It's that he knew if he told them that they wouldn't learn. Many of the most important areas of growth are caught more than taught. Jesus used parables to draw people into an immersion experience. He taught humility once the disciples started fighting over who was the best. He taught persevering prayer when they kept falling asleep. He taught service with a towel around his waist. He taught love through a cross.

We often have growth backwards. We tell people to sit still and listen to sermons. We somehow hope that showing up once a week will translate into life transformation. We are as mistaken as Jesus' crowds thinking they could get the *secrets of the kingdom* without following Jesus. Our misdirected growth model leads to frustrated pastors and immature attendees. I want to show you an alternative model built on a better foundation.

Six Dynamics

Communitas has a framework for cultivating church planting movements that involves six key dynamics[80]. These six verbs describe a natural process for activating sustainable, missional church from the ground up. Rather than creating contrived environments for lecture-based growth, these dynamics allow growth to happen where it is most natural—an immersion experience in Christ-centered community.

1. Embed
2. Initiate
3. Practice
4. Mature
5. Hub
6. Extend

---

[80] Daniel Steigewald, Deborah Loyd, April Te Grootenhuis Crull and Michael Kuder, *Dynamic Adventure: A Guide to Starting and Shaping Missional Churches* (Centennial, CO: Christian Associates International, 2016). Note: this section on the "Six Dynamics" was edited by the primary author, Daniel Steigerwald.

The dynamics are ordered in a natural progression from 1 to 6. However, the process is more fluid and cyclical than simple steps. For example, a church is never done *embedding* and *initiating*; the other dynamics simply build upon a culture of continual *embedding* and *initiating*. And so it goes with the rest.

The six dynamics work to promote integration of **place, people** and **practices** because they allow church to both start in culture *and* stay in culture.

1. Embed

The first dynamic is *embedding*. Whereas many church plants begin by starting a worship service and trying to attract people through marketing, Communitas begins by moving the team into the neighborhood. We discussed this process of incarnating within a culture in Chapter 9 when we talked about integrated **place**. The excellent book, *The New Parish*, refers to this as *faithful presence*.[81] This is the profound, yet simple, practice of living like Jesus in a community over the long haul and can never be replaced by cheap gimmicks or strategies. Here we exegete the culture, ask good questions, listen and discern what the good news of Jesus means specifically for this place and these people. *Embedding* implies learning to identify with the goodness and the pain of our setting, such that we become cultural insiders.

When our Nackle community wanted to impact Tacoma, we didn't start by parachuting into a random park and throwing a big attractional event. We started by purchasing homes in a neighborhood. As we moved in, renovated our houses together and lived our normal lives, we

---

[81] Paul Sparks, Tim Soerens and Dwight J. Friesen, *The New Parish* (Downers Grove, IL: IVP Books, 2014), 53.

slowly met neighbors, learned names and began to understand both the strengths and brokenness of the neighborhood.

The ministry to the Iranian immigrants mentioned in the previous chapter did not start out by posting an ad for Iranians to show up to a white expat American church planter event. No, it was much more costly than printing a mailer or a poster. It began when a refugee showed up in Glasgow in desperation. One of the church planter families, the Kurtykas, took him into their home for over a year. These church planters lived in a small duplex with one bathroom. They had three teenage kids at the time they took in an Iranian refugee. The Kurtyka family did not start with a costly event; they started with a costly sacrifice. They *embedded* themselves within culture and earned a deep trust.

2. Initiate

As you have *embedded* you have absorbed your surroundings, built the beginnings of relationships and looked for ways to both serve your neighbors and to allow your neighbors to serve you. During this process your team begins to discern where and how you can most effectively demonstrate and proclaim the message of Jesus. Taking these active steps is what it means to *initiate*.

The Kurtyka family *initiated* a Friday night meal with some of the immigrant families once the opportunity presented itself. Not only did their live-in immigrant feel blessed, but he invited his friends to come participate in this weekly time of dining in community.

In our Colorado Neighbor Church, we didn't start by inviting random people to something called Neighbor Church. We started with relationships—coaching soccer, serving together, drinking beer. Once some friends in the neighborhood actually wanted to talk about spiritual things, we *initiated* a conversation. We met on a back deck with several couples to get a feel of whether or not they would like to take part in a regular spiritual discussion group. We also sought input as to what would make the group a safe environment for everyone to share honestly.

The power of *initiation* happens when the people we are wanting to love come in contact with our faith community. As this intersection happens, evangelism and discipleship begin to take place naturally. When our Nackle community invited several of our kids' teachers to one of our group dinners, they were not only touched by our question, "How can we serve you and the school?" they were touched by the real friendships they experienced in our community.

What will *initiating* look like for you? A regular time to connect in a community garden? A morning walk once a week with a neighbor? A risky step now and then to share the essence of the gospel with a friend? We don't come in with a preconceived plan. We listen. We pray. When the time is right, we *initiate*. If you want some other great ideas for initiating, check out the book, *The Art of Neighboring*.

3. Practice

Practicing refers to visibly living out our primary values and vision as a community. This includes our manner of prayer, service, working through conflict, and engaging with scripture. Over time, we develop community rhythms that we ourselves find transformative, resisting the urge to simply adopt prepackaged discipleship programs. *Practicing* is an opportunity to experiment with how to live as good news to our particular context. It is where our being and our doing, our medium and our message, come into alignment.

Maybe during the *initiating* phase, we started a regular time of service with our neighbors. Or maybe it was a spiritual discussion group in a pub. The most important thing here is not the event we create, but the

Jesus way of life people experience as they come in contact with our community or team. This Jesus life is essential not only for helping others see and experience the gospel of the Kingdom, it is also the critical lifeblood of the team and emerging church.

Practicing cannot be overstated as it is the key to immersion growth. As people come in contact with the Christian community, they begin to catch on. They witness love, communion, service, encouragement, and they join in. They are discipled by a Jesus culture, not merely by words, sermons or classes. Here, evangelism and discipleship are one.

A great example of a community that has defined its life-giving *practices* is Michael Frost's church in Sydney, Australia. They use the acronym, BELLS[82], to describe their regular rhythms of **Bless** (generosity), **Eat** (hospitality), **Listen** (attentiveness to God's voice), **Learn** (discovery), and **Sent** (mission). New monastic communities like Uffizi Missional Order practice a rule of life. Whereas most churches revolve around a schedule of regular events, integrated churches revolve around a shared way of life.

Too often pastors try to lead people into a life that they and their staff are not experiencing for themselves. We may talk about our prayer life or our devotionals from the platform, but what people experience is our events. If people were to peek behind the curtain of our day-to-day life, they would often see an event planner's frenetic office world, not the incarnational life of Christ.

As a prayer mentor of mine, Daniel Henderson, once told me, "If it isn't working for you, don't try to export it." Unfortunately, too often

---

[82] Michael Frost, *Surprise the World: The Five Habits of Highly Missional People* (Colorado Springs: NavPress, 2016), 22.

our ministry professionals are trying to give away something they don't have.

Practicing is the key to maintaining integration of **people**. Why? Because, again, we are inviting people into our way of life, not our events. We are not separating people based on who is on stage and who isn't. We are creating a community of mutually broken people experiencing God's grace together. Leaders function more like life coaches and spiritual directors than event planners and orators. We are player-coaches who come alongside people in the midst of their life as a soul friend.

Literature on growing big churches is very unhelpful here. Instead, we rely on the wisdom of the missional church movement and spiritual formation movement. Authors such as Alan Hirsch, Michael Frost, Alan Roxborough, David Benner, Howard Baker, Morris Dirks and many others are helpful guides for changing our paradigm of leadership from the holy celebrity persona model to Jesus' life-on-life model.

4. Mature

Maturing is the process of developing over time as a unique expression of the body of Christ. At this phase, your communion with God, community with each other and mission in the world increase in their level of organization and sustainability. Remember, an integrated church is not anti-institution, it is simply a different type of institution. A church must formalize processes as to how we select elders, form leaders, add members to the community, and empower people to use their gifts in service.

Maturing has nothing to do with owning a building or hiring a full-time pastor. It has much more to do with being a committed spiritual family practicing faithful presence in the neighborhood. Once Upper Room Glasgow had a regular group of people who were part of the community, some regular rhythms around the community meal, and a growing number of people involved in leadership, they began to experience the fruit of *maturing* as a church.

The work of *maturing* is never done, and there is no right model for a church on this quest toward maturity. All forms of Christ-centered community must continually be asking the question, "What might we become when this present embryonic form of church grows into adulthood?" Remember, the base unit of church is the spiritual family. In family, variety is the norm. We maintain unity in the body of Christ by keeping the gospel central, not by making cookie-cutter churches that all look and act the same. Some will be larger, some will be smaller. Some families will gather in convention centers or concert venues, others will gather in homes or apartments. Some families will sing together, some will not. Some will pray in tongues, some will pray in silence. Some will practice a formal Eucharist, some will make the informal meal their time of communion. *Maturing* does not have one look or one liturgy or one theological soapbox.

A church's *maturing* cannot be measured by event metrics, the quality of the website or the hottest band. No, a *maturing* church is the one with the strongest relationships with God, each other and the world— as well as the infrastructure to support those relationships.[83]

5. Hub

Hubbing means moving beyond a single church community to collaborating on a wider level with other churches and networks across a city or region. The expressed purpose of *hubbing* is both the health of

---

[83] For more on this idea of discernment benchmarks to help teams set their own progress metrics for "growing up," see *Grow Where You're Planted: Collected Stories on the Hallmarks of Maturing Church*, edited by Daniel Steigerwald and Kelly Crull (Christian Associates Press: Portland OR, 2013).

the individual congregations as well as seeding new expressions of church. As people find community life valuable they want to share it with others. This fuels the desire to see similar Christ-centered communities form.

Hubbing is not always easy as it requires an intentional commitment by leadership teams to see beyond their own interests and exhibit a posture of seeking first the Kingdom in their city. Regardless, it is essential for both health and growth. Networks of churches are able to offer training, teaching and coaching opportunities that a single expression of church simply cannot maintain.

Hubbing is also one of the keys to financial sustainability for networks of smaller churches. Again, the desire is not necessarily to pay for full-time pastors. Leaders can, of course, receive some support from their community, but the main goal is to support the network as a whole, including the apostolic leaders who act as the operational glue for the *hub*.

While most individual communities will include people with gifts such as pastors, teachers, compassion and hospitality, the hub opens the door for more gifts to be employed, especially those of apostles and prophets. These outward-focused gifts provide the catalyzing leadership needed to sustain new church expressions.

6. Extend

The final dynamic is *extend*. This is the same idea as *hubbing*, but it reaches beyond the local network to establish or tap into networks in new regions, cities or even countries. This linking allows learning communities to be established across broader areas that not only inform churches in their practice, but also create opportunities to share resources and develop churches across diverse cultural populations and harder to reach areas.

A Growing Movement

Communitas is not the only organization using these types of practices. Voices all over the world speak from a similar paradigm of ministry. Other movements use slightly different language, but many of the same principles overlap. Books like *Missional Communities*[84], *The Tangible Kingdom*[85], *The New Parish*[86], *Building a Discipling Culture*[87] and *The Forgotten Ways*[88] offer great perspectives from other voices in the dialogue. Each has stories to share of kingdom movements throughout the world that operate from a fundamentally different foundation.

In addition to these examples, I have recently come in contact with a church who call themselves Tampa Underground[89]. Despite the name, they are quickly becoming more than just an underground movement. Tampa Underground is a rare church practicing the integration of all three forms—**place, people** and **practices.**

The Underground started out as a group of fifty or so friends, mostly InterVarsity workers (a parachurch ministry aimed at discipling college students). This group of friends shared a common concern for the church. They were successfully discipling students, but time after time, as their well-equipped and impassioned student leaders entered the "local church," they only found frustration. These students wanted to make an impact for Christ on their cities. Instead, they found themselves listening to sermon after sermon and being treated like just another tithing unit. This grieved the InterVarsity leaders at a deep level.

---

[84] Reggie McNeil, *Missional Communities: The Rise of the Post-Congregational Church* (San Francisco, CA: Jossey-Bass, 2011).
[85] Halter and Smay, *The Tangible Kingdom.*
[86] Sparks, Soerens and Friesen, *The New Parish.*
[87] Breen and Cockram, *Building a Discipling Culture.*
[88] Hirsch, *The Forgotten Ways.*
[89] For more of The Underground story, visit https://vimeo.com/256315051.

Some of these InterVarsity friends entered into a long season of prayer for the church, which included an extended trip to Manila, Philippines. There they observed church planting practices alongside leaders working in the slums of Manila. They came back with a revolutionary structure and set of values for a new church that would enable them to finally empower their student leaders and others to make an impact on their city, rather than sitting in pews.

Tampa Underground is structured around what they call micro-churches (MCs). They currently have over 200 MCs in their Tampa network (roughly thirteen hundred people). The smallest is a few people, the largest is over 150. If you have been asking questions regarding the scalability of integrated churches, this should answer your question. Every person in the network is a participant. Every person is a missionary. The Underground, rather than being built around a central worship gathering, is designed as a nonprofit organization that offers a suite of services used to empower their people. When a person has a burden for anything, whether it is homelessness, the sex trade, their neighborhood or poverty, Tampa Underground works to empower them.

The Underground staff assists in every step of the formation of the new micro-church. They have someone to help the new leader or team learn to budget, another person dedicated to their media presence, still another to coach and disciple them. They even offer tax help for MCs pursuing nonprofit status. All of these services enable people to listen to God's voice, form spiritual family around a cause or need, and walk together in their mission.

The Underground doesn't own a central worship complex. Instead, they rent an urban industrial space that they call The Hub. It is a coworking space that looks and runs like a business startup incubator. This allows MC leaders a place to office, host small to medium-sized gatherings, and prepare the infrastructure they need to launch more micro-churches.

The leadership model is the exact inverse of most Western churches. Most churches utilize volunteers to run the programs that the central staff create. Tampa Underground instead empowers people to run their own decentralized communities. The network contains a wide variety of MC focus areas: writers, artists, prison inmates, human trafficking victims, African-American girls and many more. It is messy. Many MCs fail. Many lessons are learned the hard way. Staff walk with leaders through their ups and downs, but they do not micromanage them. They allow people to take risks and to fail—and often to succeed beyond their wildest imagination!

In many ways you can see the InterVarsity roots in the way they are structured. Tampa Underground is a very unique blend of what has traditionally been known as *parachurch* and *local church*. While most parachurch ministries do a great job structuring themselves for mission, they do not think of themselves as a church community. Tampa fills in this missing gap by creating a sense of community among its MCs. Many MC leaders are also elders within the larger community and many go through an additional ordination process. While MCs each have a missional component to their existence, they also focus on communing with God and with each other.

Tampa Underground is a beautiful picture of integration. They have integrated their **place**. Tampa, Florida, is blessed by the presence of over a thousand missionaries being salt and light to every part of society imaginable. Their footprint on the community is not an impressive building or costly event, but instead countless lives touched by Christ. They are truly doing church within culture.

They have integrated their **people**. The entire network is a community of mutual participation. Church is an *all-play*. Executive Director Brian

Sanders speaks at their large leadership summits that they run every year, but he is not a celebrity. The heroes are the people doing the work of the ministry in every dark corner of the city. If anything, Brian is famous for empowering others, not for drawing attention to himself. He takes no salary from the church. He fundraises everything he receives. In fact, the entire church budget is only around $800K per year for a church of thirteen hundred people. Amazingly enough, they actually give away 60 percent of that budget toward special grants for their MCs and international partners working with the poorest of society. Most of their budget comes from a once-a-year pledge from their community, not from worship service tithe money. Almost all of their staff are bi-vocational leaders.

Finally, the network has integrated their **practices**. They do offer a weekly medium-sized gathering for people in their network, but this is not the main focus. It is also not connected to their financial model. It is only an optional gathering for people that want the extra teaching. Most of the staff focus goes toward the MCs. Because of this, the Underground is free from the mixed motives of the fee-for-service financial model. They don't need to set themselves up as the stars or keep anyone dependent on them for spiritual food. They are free to devote their lives to equipping the saints for the works of the ministry. This blend of smaller size, life-on-life community, and missional focus allows participants to taste holistic worship together.

I asked Jeremy Stephens, the Associate Director, about the sustainability of the Underground. He said, "Matt, that's the best part. The depth of relationship that people have by living out their calling together in tight community is something that hip branding and big salaries would never give us."

People are sticking to the network because they are part of a family, not because of clever marketing.

Their numbers are growing and they aren't even trying to grow. More than three hundred people came to Christ last year through their various MCs. The word is getting out and many people are now coming to the Underground looking for help in starting their own networks. There are now fourteen sister movements in seven different countries including Germany, Ireland and Haiti. The second largest network is in Manila with more than one hundred MCs. Birmingham, Alabama, has more than forty.

Tampa Underground is practicing the Six Dynamics. They use some different language, but it is the same foundation. They are a network of people, not church services. Their center of worship is wherever their people are, not an event in a building. They are deeply **embedded** in Tampa, Florida. They are **initiating** justice where God reveals a need. They are **practicing** faithful presence in their city. Many of their MCs are **mature** expressions of church. The network grows locally as they **hub** together and globally as they **extend** into new cities and countries.

The Medium and the Message

In the first chapter of this book, I opened with an illustration about the medium and the message. I said that most of our modern Western churches are using temple media. We are using forms that speak of separation while the gospel speaks of radical integration. We are treating church as if it is **a holy place where holy people do holy things.**

In Tampa, Florida, that is no longer the case. In Tampa, people are hearing the gospel, not just in word, but in the very structure of Tampa Underground. The medium and the message are one and the same. And the city is listening.

The same is true of the Communitas churches scattered throughout the world. Madrid is hearing the gospel message loud and clear, as are Santa Barbara, Glasgow and many other cities. The gospel speaks of God made flesh. That same God who sent Christ as the living temple into the mess of culture is still sending his church into his beautiful yet broken garden as the living temple.

These churches are churches in exile—churches without their own place worshipping God in every place. Like the woman at the well, they no longer need to go to a building to find their God. They have returned to *the everywhere worship of Eden.*

If you have been wondering if the church you are dreaming of is possible, the answer is yes. It's not about one organization, one name, one perfect model. It's not about Tampa Underground or Communitas.

It's about all of us.

We don't have to keep doing what we've been doing. We can experience an integrated church for ourselves.

Hope for the Established Church

I know this is a stretch for many. I know it can feel overwhelming. If you are pastoring an existing congregation, you are not going to be able to just preach a few great new sermons and have your congregation get it. We are dealing with a different wineskin. And new wine often bursts old wineskins.

Clearly, I have a strong bias. I am writing about the failure of our buildings and media to create the type of Christian culture of disciples that the world needs. Does that mean there is no possibility of your existing congregation getting a taste of holistic worship? Of course not. There are incremental steps you can take in order to move worship out of the *fourth place* and into reality. As we have discussed with our other media, there are three main directions to choose.

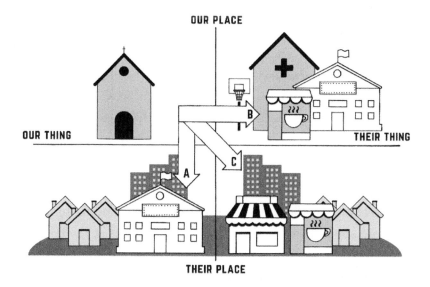

A. OUR THING, THEIR PLACE

If you are an existing church and you are not yet communicating to your congregation that what happens in the small group is just as much part of church as what happens at the building, you are missing out. Consider writing a complete list of church functions and seeing just how many you can move from the building into the small groups. Pastoral care. Visitation. Communion. Baptism. Taking care of physical needs. Bible study. Prayer. You name it, you can move it from the *fourth place* into the *first place*, the home. As you do, your medium begins to speak of holistic worship.

B. THEIR THING, OUR PLACE

What if instead of paying money for an associate pastor to teach classes, you hired someone to turn some of your usable space into a coworking business? What if instead of hiring a youth pastor, you hired a community center director? What if instead of running a youth group of a few church kids, you let Young Life use your facility and minister to a hundred kids from the local high school?

What is the best use of your resources? We are so accustomed to hiring church people to do church things that sometimes we can't think outside our *fourth place* box. When we begin to use our facility for organizations and purposes outside the religious zone, we affirm all of life as worship. When our staff has a mix of theological and business acumen, we start to think differently about ministry.

C. THEIR THING, THEIR PLACE

Jesus entered our world. Jesus taught about money and farming. Jesus cared more about justice in Jerusalem than sacrifices at the temple. If we are going to move toward holistic worship we are going to need to repent of our addiction to performance excellence and shift toward a culture of mercy. How? By decreasing dependence on the show and increasing dependence on relationship. By changing the financial model. If we can bring in money through legitimate business instead of Christian entertainment, we no longer need to feed our rampant consumerism.

If we want to help people experience all of life as worship, we are going to have to limit the complexity and expense of our events. We need to get way less excited about new gear for the worship team and way more excited about caring for the people in our cities.

An Uphill Battle

Admittedly, moving toward holistic worship as a building-centered church is a big challenge. Yes, there are incremental steps you can take, but it will be very difficult to change your culture as far as you may want to go. As long as you meet in a large auditorium facing a stage with a giant screen, your media are designed for a certain type of church experience. They lend toward a certain type of leader. They naturally demand a certain level of performance excellence. Holy places lead to holy people which lead to holy practices. They are all linked together.

That is why I want to push you to consider a new paradigm. Do what God tells you to do, but pray! We need people to leave the *fourth place* behind and join a movement toward spiritual family. It will cost you something. You will not be a part of the hip church in your city anymore. You will not feel like you are a part of something big and impressive. It will probably feel awkward at first. Events can feel clean and polished; real people are messy.

When I was talking to Jeff Shaffer who heads up the Uffizi Missional Order in Santa Barbara, I asked him if he misses worship services. His response: "There are times that I do. But then I attend one and honestly, it just doesn't feel like it's real anymore. I don't know how to explain it, but I feel closer to God—like I'm really worshiping—when I am serving food to my friends without homes in Pershing Park."

What about you?

Are you willing to trade something neat and polished and expensive for something dirty but real? Are you okay with leaders that don't have all of the answers because they've stopped pretending?

Will you be okay when it starts to grate on you that performance standards have dropped? Will you be content knowing that we are giving money away instead of upgrading our gear? Will you judge your leaders for their lack of professionalism? Are you going to be okay interacting with annoying people you don't always like? Sometimes it's nice to be alone in a crowd.

I don't want to make this transition sound more glorious than it is. Honestly, Constantine's church looks a lot more impressive and fun on the outside than Jesus' church. There is a cost to giving up the *fourth place*.

Are you ready for that?

Preaching in Context

Some of you feel ready, and nevertheless you still may be wondering, "If I let go of the *fourth place*, am I letting go of good preaching?" Let's end this chapter with an encouragement for those of you who thought I wanted to do away with the word of God.

In Chapter 9, I mentioned the Starbucks training methodology—70 percent on-the-job training, 20 percent mentoring, and 10 percent content. We don't have hard data on the exact percentages, but this sounds pretty similar to Jesus and his followers. Most of their time was spent in real life together—on the road, at meals, caring for hurting people. This is the 70 percent. It is Jesus' discipleship immersion experience, Jesus' on-the-job training.

However, Jesus didn't let them go through their immersion alone. He talked with them, he debriefed with them, he challenged them. This is the 20 percent mentoring component. Finally, yes, Jesus spoke. He spoke to crowds. He was known as *rabbi*—teacher. Some of his teaching came one-on-one, some in small groups, and some to the multitudes. This is the 10 percent content.

Our churches have these ratios backwards. Our primary activity is sermons. The pastor spends the bulk of his or her week preparing content. We don't have time for mentoring and one-on-one discipleship, and we don't even have a clue what "on-the-job training" would even look like other than showing people how to run events.

Hopefully, by this point, after hearing the stories of integrated church communities, you have a better idea of what "on-the-job training" means. It is the immersion the Iranian man experienced during his year living in the same home as the church planters. It is a micro-church dedicating its after work hours to getting yet one more woman off the streets and out of the sex trade. It is a random, unplanned meal with someone in the neighborhood. It is normal life together in culture.

That is our primary way to grow. That is the 70 percent. That is immersion. We have also talked about the 20 percent—a new model of leadership that allows pastors to be more like coaches and spiritual directors than wedding planners.

Now I want to address the 10 percent. The content. Jesus taught. Paul taught. Paul commanded Timothy to preach the word. When you are on mission with people, when you are sharing life, a timely sermon is like a drink of cold water in the desert. You thirst for it. It feeds the soul. When you have deeply loving and committed relationships, you can take that word and process it together. When 90 percent is real life together, you hunger for the 10 percent.

I have argued that the church in the West is like a family that gave up all of the normalness of family life in exchange for running weddings every weekend. True, but weddings still have their place.

A Timely Wedding

When families are close, when they care deeply about each other in normal life, there is nothing more beautiful than a wedding. When we are experiencing the substance of real family, it actually makes sense from time to time to get dressed up, hire a professional orator, have Uncle Larry sing a solo, and get some volunteers to help with parking. It is the same with the church. When we are truly a spiritual family on mission together, a timely event can ignite a fire in our community.

Young Life takes its kids away to camp once a year. Tampa Underground runs a leadership summit annually to speak into the lives of their leaders. Communitas has global summits, regional gatherings, and ongoing learning opportunities within hubs and church networks.

Trained people run these events—people with deep theological backgrounds and real seminary degrees.

Sometimes we need to get outside the boundaries of our small spiritual family. Sometimes we need a good conference. Sometimes we need a retreat. Sometimes we need a whole weekend dedicated to understanding a book of the Bible at a deeper level. There is a place in these contexts for excellent preaching and teaching. There is a place for long hours of preparation for a talk. Yes, there may even be a place for a great worship band.

These are not our weekly rhythms, however. These are special events. These are the weddings.

How often should we throw these types of events? As often as it is helpful. As often as it builds people toward being better disciples within their spiritual families, without the events taking the place of their spiritual families. There is no easy answer here. We should be gracious with the efforts of any community that is honestly trying to figure this balance out for their network.

To move forward as a church who connects with God and others in all spheres of life, we must continually ask ourselves the question, "Are we investing our time and energy running events and building our own kingdoms, or are we giving our lives away in radical mercy to God's beloved garden?" We are all worshipers. Let's make sure we are worshiping *outside the camp* with Christ, not at the altar of the *fourth place*.

Closing Encouragements

Friends, we are living through a radical paradigm shift in ministry. We have talked at length now about moving toward integration instead of separation. While you may be excited about all of the new possibilities and ideas that may be opening up for you, I want to leave you with a few words of optimistic caution.

We should not expect everyone to adopt the new (older) paradigm right away. Instead, we should expect most of our communities to still be deeply rooted in their traditions. Even many of the people who are trying new structures of church still have a deep longing for large corporate worship. They miss it. It feels wrong to them not to attend services and listen to sermons every week. Why? Because they've done it their whole life!

This is no different from the days of John Calvin when former Catholics moved forward under Protestantism, but did so with optimistic yet heavy hearts. Calvin was continually frustrated with large numbers of people who would mumble in Latin during his sermons.[90] We think a cell phone going off is bad! Why were they doing it? They didn't even understand Latin! Yet it still felt comfortable because they grew up with it, and they missed it.

Traditions, even bad ones, are not easily broken.

Alan Hirsch compares changes of medium to learning to drive on the other side of the road. It is scary at first. Uncomfortable. Unsettling. Still, if that's the lane you need to be in to avoid oncoming traffic, it will start to settle in.

I pray the same thing for the church—that we can eventually settle into some forms that keep us from the constant collisions with ourselves.

---

[90] Robert Kingdom, "Worship in Geneva Before and After the Reformation" in Karin Maag and John D. Witvliet, Editors, *Worship in Medieval and Early Modern Europe: Change and Continuity in Religious Practice* (Notre Dame, Indiana: University of Notre Dame Press, 2004), 54.

Some of you may read this book and feel deeply called of God to burst the *fourth place* wineskin and move forward with boldness in a network of spiritual families. Others, God may call to move slower—to take more pastoral care of their existing congregations without quickly alienating people that God loves. Some of you with existing buildings may feel obligated, even called, to sell them and invest your lives in a relational network. You should not expect this transition to be easy nor intuitive for those who join with you. On the contrary, we should expect change of this nature to rub against everything people have been raised to think is normal behavior of good Christians.

Be optimistic. But be aware. There is room in the body of Christ for slow change. For pastoral care, love and patience. There is also room for taking risks. For boldness. For a new season of church. This is also love.

I want to encourage you as I close to take a step. Ask God what that step might be. Take the time needed to listen to the Father. Process this book in community with people you trust.

We have a big problem in the church, probably bigger than we realize. Our forms are not in line with our function. Our media are speaking a message of separation, while the great gospel of our Lord Jesus is bursting at the seams to speak its own message of radical integration.

When Jesus came to earth he left his own place and entered our world. It's time that we followed him there.

It's time to get *out of the fourth place.*

AFTERWORD

I want to invite you to join the conversation.

I would love to hear how you are processing and living out this material. Go to www.outofthe4thplace.com to share your own thoughts and experiences, read blogs on related topics and purchase more books.

Even better than online conversations, I want to encourage you to start a real conversation with a friend. Buy them a copy of this book and chew on it together (not literally, that'd be gross). Whether in a *third place* over a coffee, a *second place* over a TPS report, a *first place* around a fireplace, or even a *fourth place* around an organ, we need to talk about this stuff and dream together.

Grab a friend, your book club, your team or your staff and let's talk.

To buy more copies, Amazon is great. For a better deal, especially for bulk orders, you can order from www.outofthe4thplace.com. Either way, all proceeds from book sales go toward planting and supporting churches outside of the *fourth place*.

Matt Broweleit

Printed in Great Britain
by Amazon

33211310R00158